The
Highway Code
for Happiness

The
Highway Code
for Happiness

Michael & Hilary Perrott

Concept development, editing, design and production by CWR

Printed in Croatia by Zrinski

ISBN: 978-1-85345-485-1

About happiness

The ads proclaim it, universities teach it, everyone wants it. Why then do so many not find it – lastingly? Perhaps because they don't look in the right place.

Happiness is not a state of continual bliss in which there are no tears and where no pain is felt. Nor does it wear a permanent grin. It knows disappointment, yet finds contentment; it experiences life's blows, but remains resilient. It is experienced most fully where values are upheld and responsibilities met. At its core are unselfishness and service.

Happiness does not just happen. Our lives are shaped largely not by circumstances, but by –

> **A**ttitudes we adopt
> **B**eliefs we hold
> **C**hoices we make

In writing *The Highway Code for Happiness* we have drawn on the many years we have been involved in counselling men and women from all walks of life, sharing their sorrows as well as their joys. The book itself was written while we were recovering from a major road accident, and while Michael was receiving treatment for a life-threatening illness.

We have found that life is best when balanced; where mind and emotion dovetail, where character and relationships go hand in hand, and where the physical and spiritual combine in a whole person.

Happiness is a serious business!

Michael and Hilary Perrott

Contents

Contents

Searching for happiness

¹2m

unmet longing; life needs
meaning; where are we going?

Searching for happiness

HAPPINESS IS WITHIN. Some people have everything, yet are miserable, others have little or nothing, but are content and full of vitality. What makes the difference? The latter have found that what *happens* in their world, however hard, need not ultimately control how they feel, and they have discovered that what happens *in* them is more important than what happens *to* them. *What we are* affects *what we feel*, so happiness (or unhappiness) is, at least in part, our choice.

Unmet longing

WHO IN THE WORLD DOES NOT WANT TO BE HAPPY? The desire is so deep that as the body needs breath, so the heart craves happiness. Why then is this universal longing so often unmet?

Why? The answer lies in the very nature of happiness. A child who tries to catch his own shadow will always be empty-handed. As he runs, the shadow runs from him. But let him turn and face the sun and run towards it, and he finds his shadow follows him. Seek happiness for *itself*, and it escapes us. But if we aim for other, better, higher things, we are more likely to find it. We can discover happiness when we are not looking for it!

MEMO

We can discover happiness when we are not looking for it!

The longing for happiness is natural, but if we make it the main purpose of our lives, if we pursue it doggedly with no thought of others, of right and wrong or of consequences, we will be sorely disappointed. By all means let us prize happiness, but never as a first prize. C.S. Lewis was right when he said, 'You can't get second things by putting them first; you can get second things only by putting first things first.' It is the same principle as that given by Jesus in another context, '… seek first his kingdom and his righteousness, and all these things will be given to you as well.'[1]

If we make happiness our main goal in life, then everything – work, family, even God – will merely be a means of making us happy. We won't find a great purpose by pursuing happiness; we are much more likely to find happiness by pursuing a great purpose, even in the face of tragedy.

IN THE FACE OF TRAGEDY. A seventeen-year-old girl took, she says, 'a reckless dive into what I thought was deep water. But my head hit the bottom and it snapped my neck.' In hospital she thought, 'Oh God, my life's over. I want to die.'

Later she said, 'I'm paralysed in all four limbs. My hands don't work … I haven't walked a step in years.' It takes two hours each morning for someone to get her up, to go through the toilet routines, get her dressed, exercised and strapped into her wheelchair. For her to blow her nose someone has to press her abdomen as she only has fifty per cent lung capacity. But when a teenage girl asked, 'But now you're happy?', she answered, 'I really am. I wouldn't change my life for anything.' Can anyone with problems like that really be happy? As we shall see in this book, they can.

WHAT IS HAPPINESS? Definition is difficult, for happiness is subjective, and like love, is better 'felt than telt'. But it is not the same as –

o **Pleasure**. Words like enjoyment, bliss, ecstasy and pleasure describe emotions which fade, often quickly, and may be experienced in a very unhappy life. Drugs give pleasure *now* – and misery later. A 'happy hour' is what it says – a happy hour. Happiness is deeper than pleasure.

o **Relief**. A person will be 'happy' to get relief from toothache, to have passed an exam or to escape from a difficult situation. But relief from pain is usually temporary and no guarantee of a fulfilling life. Happiness is more than relief.

o **Blessing**. The word 'blessed', as in the teaching of Jesus, 'Blessed are the merciful …',[2] describes *how God sees people* not *how people feel*. If people are happy it is not so much because they are merciful but because they are blessed by God (that is they have His gracious favour). Happiness is a result of blessedness.

What, then, is happiness? Dictionaries stumble and miss the mark, for happiness is something *experienced* rather than *explained*. Pleasure (or displeasure) is what we *feel* at any given moment, while happiness is satisfaction as we *think* about our life. Some people compare it unfavourably to joy and dismiss happiness as superficial. But the words are largely interchangeable. The student is 'happy' or 'overjoyed' at the result of his exam, and the parent 'happy' or 'full of joy' over the birth of the baby. It is only in the chapter 'Growing in spirit' (see page 75) that we find there is a joy which can be described as happiness with a deeper dimension.

FACTS ABOUT HAPPINESS

o **Parents.** Biological parents pass on certain traits to their children. If we have inherited a happy disposition we have had a good start. But if we haven't, that does *not* mean we cannot be happy. We can't change the shape of our nose (except by surgery) but we *can* change our outlook on life. That's a choice.

o **Early years.** The formative years are enormously important, and the child who is loved and encouraged is fortunate. But even when there has been abuse and rejection, where there is strong resolve, especially with outside help, it is possible to find happiness.

o **Circumstances.** The word 'happy' is derived from the Old Norse *happ* meaning luck or good fortune, but whereas circumstances, good or bad, influence the way we feel, they do not control it. If we look at adverse circumstances as a challenge rather than a misfortune, we will go about changing them if we can or handling them if we can't. The apostle Paul, beaten, stoned, imprisoned and shipwrecked; cold, hungry and naked; lived in danger both from man and nature. But he was able to say, '… I have learned to be content whatever the circumstances.' [3]

Some of the happiest people live *permanently* in the toughest situations. Helen Keller, blind and deaf from when she was a baby, became a widely travelled and world-famous speaker and author. She wrote, 'A happy life consists not in the absence, but in the mastery of hardships.'

 'A happy life consists not in the absence, but in the mastery of hardships' | MEMO

o **Money.** Once the basic necessities of life are met – food, clothing and shelter – there is little to choose between income groups as to their experience of happiness. Why? Because many find the more they have the more they want. Wealth is comparative:

even the rich don't always feel rich, if richer 'Joneses' have what they don't. Lottery winners, once the excitement of winning has worn off, are often as happy or unhappy as they were before their win. No wonder Jesus said, 'Life is not defined by what you have, even when you have a lot.'[4] Having a lot to live on is nothing compared to having a lot to live for.

○ **Sex.** No one would deny the contribution to happiness that sex makes when expressed in the security of commitment and loyalty. But sex for the sake of sex is highly unsatisfactory. It leaves behind a trail of misery; sexually transmitted infections, unwanted pregnancies, abortions; the loss of self-respect and dignity; blame, guilt and emotional turmoil; broken hearts and broken homes. Sex may excite, but in itself does not bring happiness.

○ **Work.** Although pay is important, it is not as big an influence on job satisfaction as relationships at work, and the nature of the work itself. Noel Coward famously quipped that interesting work is 'more fun than fun'. A person's feelings are affected by how much they have control over what they do, and if they lose their job the loss of self-respect may impact them as much as loss of income.

○ **Religion.** Surveys consistently show that people for whom God is important report being significantly happier than those for whom he is not. Why? They are more likely to have a sense of purpose in life, a buffer against its storms and concerns beyond their own interests.

○ **Attitude.** Attitude is a major factor in happiness. Those with a positive attitude choose to look up not down, forwards not backwards. They look for the best in others, and resolve to be the best themselves. Their effort matters to them even if the results are not what they hoped for. They choose cheerfulness, not whingeing; gratitude, not complaining. When they fail, they start again. They have a positive 'happitude' to life. Abraham Lincoln summed it up when he remarked, 'Most people are about as happy as they make up their minds to be.'

A SERIOUS BUSINESS. What makes for happiness is examined in these pages. The authors hold a Christian world-view, but invite those who may not share it to join them in exploring the values which make for wholeness. Here is no empty promise of some magic 'ten easy steps to happiness'. There are no quick fixes or short cuts. Rather, we will find that dreams need discipline, contentment comes through character and it is meaning that makes life worthwhile. Happiness is a serious business!

> **Happiness is a serious business!**
>
> MEMO

Life needs meaning

The average person today is no happier than people fifty years ago. Everything is more, bigger and better, and life itself is longer, yet the enjoyment of life is no greater. Why? Because without meaning there is no lasting happiness. Some find meaning in –

- **Achievement (doing)** – the satisfaction that comes from reaching a goal
- **Ambition (being)** – the importance of achieving position or standing
- **Acquisition (having)** – the possession of money or material things
- **Acceptance (belonging)** – the respect or love which is longed for

There may, of course, be a combination of these. In themselves all are legitimate aims, but when centred on self, many confess there is something still missing. A man in mid-life summed it up when he drew a circle round his chest and murmured, 'There is a hole inside me.' His mind was active, his body fit, but as he said himself, his spirit was dead. Neglect the inside, and the outside is just a shell. But when security, self-worth and significance are met in God, life takes on a new meaning. Augustine, who left his stamp upon the centuries, was right when he said, 'O God, you have made us for yourself, and our hearts are restless until they rest in you.' A circle needs a centre.

| MEMO | 'O God, you have made us for yourself, and our hearts are restless until they rest in you' |

For happiness to be ongoing there needs to be a good *end* in sight, but also a *means* to that end. As one person explained, 'For me happiness comes not only from what lies on the horizon, but on the road that leads me there. I need both the NOW and the THEN.' To be truly happy, journey and destination must both be worthwhile.

MEANINGLESS MEN. Achievement, ambition, acquisition, acceptance – he had it all, and to a degree it is almost impossible to grasp. He was a prolific writer and composer, famed for his giant intellect, and in his day probably the richest man in the world. Magnificently housed, he created beautiful parks, owned sprawling farms and had a thousand women to satisfy his insatiable libido. His every word was law.

But was he happy? Let him speak for himself. 'I denied myself nothing my eyes desired; I refused my heart no pleasure.' He went on, 'Yet when I surveyed all that my hands had done and what I had toiled to achieve, everything was meaningless, a chasing after the wind; nothing was gained under the sun.' [5] Like the boy vainly chasing his shadow, King Solomon found that his search for happiness was like chasing the wind. He had one word for it: meaningless. If ever there was a man who worked hard at climbing a ladder and then found it was leaning against the wrong wall, it was Solomon.

In the mid twentieth century the swashbuckling playboy actor Errol Flynn excited the imagination and envy of the world. But in his book *My Wicked, Wicked Ways* he admits, 'I had wealth, friends, I was internationally known, I was sought after by women. I could have anything money could buy. Yet I found that at the top of the world there was nothing. I was sitting on a pinnacle, with no mountain under me.'

The world had not changed in 3,000 years: the king found the way he was living had no meaning; the playboy found that when he had everything, he had nothing.

HAPPY ALL THE TIME? Can everyone be happy all the time? No! There are children, terribly abused, who have no means of defending themselves. There are people living under severe oppression, suffering the ravages of starvation, facing slow or violent death. Even in countries with stable governments and economies, there are the highs and lows of life that all must face. There are battles to fight and tears to shed. The happy are not without heartache. There is loss and loneliness, disappointment, grief and pain, which basically happy people may feel as keenly as the unhappy. But because they are 'whole', because life has meaning, they find it easier to ride the storms.

A person needs difficulties to face and obstacles to overcome or they would not be happy. Life would be too simple – and too dull. A land which was all sun and had no rain would die. It is the rain that falls which makes us glad to see the sun. A life too easy will have no joy.

A life too easy will have no joy

A RIGHT TO HAPPINESS? We may wish a 'Happy Birthday' to someone or they a 'Happy New Year' to us, and hopefully their wish and ours will come true, but a wish is not a right. A right to happiness is like saying we have a right to riches or a right to be married. We may want both but can demand neither, for no one has a duty to provide us with wealth or agree to marry us. Nor do we have the right to pursue happiness in any way we like. Does a paedophile have a right to abuse children just because doing so gives him pleasure? Does a person on a high through drink or drugs have a right to drive a car and kill someone? No! If happiness is found it is because of responsibilities which are met, not rights which are claimed.

Where are we going?

We look at the guide map and the red dot announces, 'You are here'. Does that describe us? We are creatures of time and eternity. Life here is important but we must never become so preoccupied with it that we forget that there is another world. If we don't know how to live life, or care where we are going, then we may do well to remember the conversation between Alice and the Cheshire Cat.

> Alice, 'Would you tell me, please, which way I
> ought to go from here?'
> Cat, 'That depends a good deal on where you
> want to get to.'
> Alice, 'I don't much care where.'
> Cat, 'Then it doesn't matter which way you go.'

Clever cat! We want a good life? Then it matters how we live it. The Greek philosopher Plato hit the mark when he said, 'There is no question which a man of any sense could take more seriously than … what kind of life we should live.'

It's been said that, 'The mind, body and soul are very close neighbours, and one usually catches the ills of the others.' They do, very easily, and we might add feelings, character and relationships. But when all these are in good health they also affect each other positively.

'The good life' (so-called) is nothing compared to being *good at life*, and that means handling life well. To do this we must begin with the mind. That's where we think, where we believe, where we choose. Our life is shaped by our thoughts, by images and by words unspoken which race through our brain. Change our thinking and we can change. These pages are about us, those parts of us that make up the whole. They are about happiness, not as an aim but as an outcome of how we think and feel, about the character we build, our body and spirit and how we relate to others. It's possible we may find our life changes forever.

> 'The good life' … is nothing compared to being *good at life*
>
> MEMO

NOTES

1. Matthew 6:33
2. Matthew 5:7
3. Philippians 4:11
4. Luke 12:15, *The Message*
5. Ecclesiastes 2:10–11

Managing the mind

^{1}2m

understanding ourselves; training
the mind; stress and de-stress;
dreams, goals and plans

Managing the mind

Attitudes matter more than facts is a principle that has turned many lives around, as can be seen dramatically in the life of Victor Frankl. A psychiatrist and Jew, he lost his wife, brother and parents in the Nazi death camps. He himself was tortured and never knew when his own life would end. But one day, naked and alone, he became aware that he had power where he had no power. He could not change his environment but he could choose how it affected him.

Frankl later wrote, 'Everything can be taken from a man but one thing, the last of human freedoms – to choose one's attitude in any given set of circumstances.' That attitude, which helped him survive the camps, enabled him to 'find hope amid despair, beauty amid desolation and nobility amid depravity'.

The mind can lead or mislead; it can believe truth or lies; it has potential for good or evil; it can be used or wasted. It is of such importance that Jesus taught that love for God is to be 'with all your mind'.[1]

MEMO

Attitudes matter more than facts

Understanding ourselves

ACCEPTING OURSELVES. Unhappiness is guaranteed for the person who keeps complaining 'If only …'.

- **Parents**. 'If only I had different parents' is a wish as pointless as it is impossible to fulfil. We can change our jeans but not our genes. There may have been failures in the way our parents (or other adults) brought us up, but we can't undo nature or unwind nurture.

- **Appearance.** Many say, 'If only I were taller (or smaller) and better-looking, life would be different.' Maybe, maybe not. It is what we *do* with what we have that is important. There are people who are not 'good-looking' but are nonetheless attractive because of dress, grooming and healthy eating. Estée Lauder of cosmetics fame used to say, 'There is no such thing as an ugly woman, only a lazy one!'

- **Personality.** Some think, 'If only I were more of an extrovert (or introvert or whatever) I would find things easier.' But it is futile thinking, for personality is largely inborn and does not alter substantially throughout life. There are no 'good' or 'bad' personalities: they are just different. It is what we *do* with our personality that matters. Our personality is a given, our character is made – by ourselves.

- **Gifts**. A gift or talent, such as an ear for music, an eye for beauty or a burst of speed, is something we either have or haven't got. Instead of saying, 'If only I had their gifts', let us use the gifts we do have, and develop them as much as we can. Many encounter failure on their way to finding their gifts. Winston Churchill twice failed to get into the Royal Military Academy at Sandhurst and Albert Einstein failed his first attempt at the entrance examination to the Polytechnic in Zurich.
  Instead of 'if only', let's accept what we are and use what we have, and we will be on the way to being happier people.

BEING HONEST WITH OURSELVES. It is good to step back and take a cool look at ourselves, acknowledging our strengths and admitting weaknesses.

o **Strengths.** While we won't boast of our strengths, it is not immodest to acknowledge them. Are we good listeners, do we encourage, take integrity seriously and finish tasks we start? Whatever the list, there are strengths which are characteristic of us and we feel glad when we exercise them. To live a full life we need to harness our strengths.

o **Weaknesss.** Are we short on discipline, quick in temper, slow to fulfil our promises? Perhaps we might follow the example of C.S. Lewis who said that, 'For the first time I examined myself with a seriously practical purpose.' He went on, 'and what I found appalled me; a zoo of lusts, a bedlam of ambitions, a nursery of fears, a harem of fondled hatreds.'[2] His self-examination was a step on the path that led to transformation. Honesty makes change possible.

TALKING TO OURSELVES. Our feelings are not caused by circumstances but by what we *tell* ourselves about those circumstances. So let's watch our language! Here are some examples of 'bad' language. If we say –

o 'He makes me mad', we are saying, 'It's his fault; I'm not responsible.'
o 'That's me. That's the way I am', we are saying, 'I can't help myself; I'm not responsible.'
o 'If only the situation were different', we are saying, 'I'm not free to be myself; I'm not responsible.'

Positive thinking does not mean psyching ourselves up by saying over and over again, 'Every day, in every way, I'm getting better and better'. That, frankly, is nonsense. Optimism must be grounded in reality. But it does mean being proactive. Stephen Covey in his *7 Habits of Highly Effective People*[3] points out that reactive people are affected by their environment. If the weather is good they feel good, and if their 'social weather' is positive and people treat them well, they feel well. But he insists 'proactive people can carry their own weather with them'.

Polish immigrant Michael Marks sold buttons and pins door-to-door, and then set up a market stall with the slogan, 'Don't ask the price – it's a penny'. The facts of his life were poverty and mastering a different language, but he looked beyond the facts and Marks & Spencer was born. Hope and hard work is a recipe for success.

Hope and hard work is a recipe for success

MEMO

Some people are naturally optimistic, but all can choose to be. The more we use the decisive 'I will do it' instead of the 'if only' of complaint and blame, the more we will develop an optimistic outlook. The more optimistic we are the more likely we are to get started on any given task. Mood-enhancing chemicals are released in the brain, and as we attack what seemed mountainous we find we get through it more easily than we thought. Successful people focus on *solutions* rather than *problems*, while the unsuccessful dwell on *problems* rather than *solutions*.

CHANGING OURSELVES

There are no short cuts to change. The apostle Paul spells out that we are to 'be transformed by the renewing of your mind'.[4] That will mean honesty which admits that change is needed, choice which takes the first step, effort which maintains the new way, and perseverance which continues in spite of obstacles and setbacks. In a different context, here is an example of change.

One day at school a boy of eight had rhubarb for lunch. Down it went, and up it came – splash! From that day he always said, 'I can't eat rhubarb.' Forty years had passed when a woman in kindness baked a rhubarb tart for him as a treat. He was too embarrassed to refuse. Down it went and … it stayed down … just. He began to think – 'Can't? But I have just done it, so I can! I didn't like it, but I did it. I'll try it again.' So he did it again … and again … and again, until it actually became a dessert of choice. He laughed, 'I am still amazed that the taste (or distaste) of forty years could be changed like that.'

A choice that takes a moment can become a change that lasts for life, and the principle is the same whether it's rhubarb or character.

MEMO

A choice that takes a moment can become a change that lasts for life

Training the mind

A man walked along a beach looking for a good place to swim. He saw a notice which announced, 'Danger. No swimming'. He pulled off his clothes, hung them on the notice board, dived in, and never came out. What possessed him? Was it pride – 'I know better'? Rebelliousness that said, 'Rules, who wants rules?' Was his mind unhinged? Apparently not. But one thing is certain, at least in any meaningful way he didn't *think*.

Our lives are shaped by our thoughts, so nothing is more important than learning to use our minds. We train the mind by being –

OPEN-MINDED. This does not mean our minds are a bin for every crazy notion, or that we have no strong convictions, but it does mean that unlike the narrow-minded we are willing to listen and want to learn.

o **Listening.** Prejudice closes the mind, listening opens it. We need to be aware of the world we live in and listen to people we don't agree with. We may conclude they have a point, but even if we don't, at least we will know how they think, and that's important.

o **Learning**. There isn't enough time in one life to learn everything by trial and error, so let's learn life lessons from others. We might become writers! That is, we write down things we have learned, for we are more likely to remember what we record. Writing helps thinking. Dawson Trotman, founder of The Navigators, wisely said, 'Thoughts disentangle themselves when they pass through your fingertips.'

 'Thoughts disentangle themselves when they pass through your fingertips' MEMO

SINGLE-MINDED. 'Things that matter most,' said Goethe, 'must never be at the mercy of things that matter least.' Let's get our priorities right and maintain them by –

o **Setting clear goals**. A goal is not just a desire, but a desire that has a target. People who set clear goals are more likely to succeed than those who don't.
   Goals help us achieve because we know what we are aiming at. But also, if we lose our way, it's easier to get back on track because we know where the track is.

○ **Being tenacious.** If ever there was a person who was single-minded it was the apostle Paul. In writing of his goal he says, 'one thing I do'.[5] He was so completely committed that he could say, '… to me, to live is Christ …'[6] No wonder coming towards the end of his life he was able to write, 'I have fought the good fight, I have finished the race, I have kept the faith.'[7]

NIMBLE-MINDED. If we look after them, our brains can stay young even when our bodies are aging. We do this by making sure we have –

○ **Variety.** Ruts are easy to get into and hard to get out of. In rural Paraguay an unpaved road had a notice in Spanish, 'Choose your rut. You're in it to the end of the road.' It is good to try new things, go new places, taste new foods, make new friends, read new books, take up a new hobby, learn a new skill. Moses was a man who left his mark on the world and he didn't begin until he was eighty! Some days we might use our left hand to open doors rather than our right, or when we put on a coat we slip a different arm into the sleeve first. We can challenge our minds by making simple changes.

○ **Activity.** We keep our minds supple with exercise. Crosswords, chess, Scrabble, Suduko, reading, talking with others, electronic games and brain training improve mental agility and memory. We need to ration the time we spend in front of the television. More fish oils, nuts and seeds, and fewer saturated fats, help keep body and brain healthily active. The more we exercise our bodies the more we challenge our brains with muscle skills and balance.

○ **Sociability.** As our lives are shaped by our thoughts, our minds are sharpened by conversation. Telling stories, swapping jokes, talking things through, doing things together with friends or family, all help to keep the mind healthy. Isolation slows the mind, interaction quickens it. A 95-year-old with the memory of a 60-year-old and the wit of a 40-year-old, when asked her secret replied, 'Friends, friends, friends.'

Isolation slows the mind, interaction quickens it

MEMO

Stress and de-stress

Everyone experiences stress. The big events of life see to that – the loss of a loved one, marriage or divorce, ill health or disability, intimidation or injustice, a different job or new neighbourhood. Stress, which is an adverse reaction to excessive or ongoing pressure, is also experienced in the everyday.

Pressure can excite, exhilarate and focus the mind, but too much for too long can leave us strained to breaking point. Of course, everyone is different, and what is stressful for one may not be for another. The following are ways in which we can 'de-stress' ourselves.

CHECKUP. The first step in dealing with stress is to take a good look at what causes it.

Identify it. Know what we are dealing with. Does it result from a difficult relationship at home or work, concerns about health or money, something that has happened or we fear might happen, or a combination of factors? We may feel tense, find it hard to sleep, relax or concentrate. Anger seethes just below the surface, depression clouds our day, aches and pains arrive for no obvious reason. Let's identify the problem and how it affects us.

- **Size it up**. Is it short-term or long-term? If it's short-term, but a task which seems huge, then a salami job when we cut it in slices and do a bit at a time, may be the best way forward. If it's long-term, then the options are *leaving it as it is*, *taking more time*, *having a different approach*, *going round it* and *facing it squarely*.

- **Take action.** *Taking more time* may be just what's needed to deal with stress coolly, carefully and comprehensively. If the present way of doing things hasn't worked, then *a different approach* may make sense. *Going round it* could sidestep an issue which in a month from now, or a year, will not matter. *Facing it squarely* will probably mean being upfront with our concerns and dealing directly with something or someone even if doing so is unpleasant.

FREE UP. Freedom comes a step at a time by doing things one at a time.

- **Plan ahead.** Stress often comes from lack of preparation. Tasks creep up on us unawares and we frantically try to meet our objective – or someone else's. So let's have two sets of time. The date when the job (or whatever) is due, and earlier than that, the date when we begin doing something about it. Having an adequate 'do date' takes stress from the last minute rush for the 'due date'. We leave a margin.

- **Clear the clutter.** A busy pastor, after many years in the ministry, said the most important lesson he had learned was, 'Be flexible with people but ruthless with paper'. Make friends with the wastepaper basket or shredder, put rubbish in the bin, take clothes to a charity shop. Clutter on desk or worktop creates clutter in the mind, just as clutter in the mind leaves its trail on desk or worktop. If we have a place for everything (and, hopefully, everything in place) we avoid the frustration of not being able to find what we need. Tidiness saves time – and stress.

'Be flexible with people but ruthless with paper'

MEMO

o **Guard your time**. Do we take on too much or accept unrealistic deadlines? Does our 'yes' bring stress? We have too much to do and too little time to do it in. The seemingly 'urgent' is not always important, and 'no' can be the most liberating word in the language. If we are not sure whether we should take on another responsibility we can say, 'Let's think about it'. It's easier to change a 'no' to a 'yes' than a 'yes' to a 'no'.

o **Write it down**. If we trust to memory alone we *will* forget something sometimes. It's list it or lose it! So let's get it out of our head and on to a pad, whether it's paper or electronic, and have the list where it is easily seen or reached. A man smiled, 'I carry my brain in my pocket!'

o **Do it now.** We can spend more energy in *not* doing something than in actually doing it. Pioneering psychologist and philosopher William James was right when he said, 'Nothing is so fatiguing as the eternal hanging on of an uncompleted task.' Procrastination is stress producing. And the opposite is true; getting something finished and out of the way gives lightness of spirit and energy for what's next.

HAND UP. Have we helped people up when they have been down? Then let's not hesitate to reach for a hand ourselves.

o **Trust a friend.** If there is stuff that bothers us, why not share it? A friend or family member may have useful advice, but even if they don't, the very act of 'getting it off our chest' is likely to help. Don't lock pain away. Many speak of the relief they have found in being understood.

MEMO

Don't lock pain away

o **Build relationships**. People can cause stress but also help it. Strong relationships lessen the tendency to brood over the past or be anxious about the future.

o **Ask for help**. Stress is experienced by all people at some time, and there is no shame in going to a doctor. Medication may be needed or time out from a situation. No one is expert in everything, and asking for help, far from being weakness, is plain common sense.

LOOK UP. Don't look backwards, look forwards; don't look down, look up.

o **Make room for fun**. To the saying, 'All work and no play makes Jack a dull boy,' might be added 'and a stressed one'. Pressure is best handled when balanced with pleasure, whatever form that takes. We should plan enjoyment. Fun is not a 'maybe' but a 'must'.

Fun is not a 'maybe' but a 'must'

MEMO

- **Laugh a bit.** Laughter needs no prescription from the doctor but is one of the best medicines. To laugh at life's ups and downs, to see the funny side of things and to laugh at ourselves, puts things in perspective. Laughter, like exercise, relaxes mind and muscle.

- **Make room for rest.** Rest may be 'feet up' rest or just 'away from work' rest. It might include recreation and leisure pursuits or time for re-creation, the recharging of spiritual batteries and refocusing on life's greater purposes.

- **Aim at fitness.** A man under great strain mentally and emotionally took up regular and vigorous walking. Laughingly he said, 'It makes me feel miles better!' With physical exercise endorphins are released into the blood, so tightness in mind and muscle is lessened. We need to take care as always with eating – what we eat, when we eat and how much we eat. The fitter we are the better we sleep, and the better we sleep the less stressed we will be.

- **Count your blessings.** There are problems to face, grief to live through and pressure to experience. We *have* to think about these things. But we don't have to dwell on them. As the quip goes, 'The secret of happiness is to count your blessings, not add up your troubles.' When we focus on the good things in life and are glad about those, we find that gratitude creates calm.

'The secret of happiness is to count your blessings, not add up your troubles'

Some recommend that we write down three things that we are glad about at the end of each day. One found, 'It's hard to be grateful and depressed at the same time', and it is widely recognised that those who express their gratitude actually have a higher quality of life. Besides, who wants to be around someone who is griping all the time? Gratitude finds friends!

o **Lift your heart.** When stress is at its worst many find prayer is best, for it brings a new dimension. There is the confidence that we will *not* be overwhelmed, for the invitation of Jesus still stands, 'Keep company with me and you'll learn to live freely and lightly.' [8]

Dreams, goals and plans

A dream is not enough, it needs a goal; a goal is not enough, it needs a plan; and a plan is not enough, it needs the will to see it through.

o **The dream.** So often dreams are never realised; they just remain – dreams. A man laughed, 'If procrastination is the thief of time then I have to admit I am a burglar! I have robbed *myself* over and over again. My desk's a mess and I'm not sure my life is much better. There are so many things I could have done, no, should have done, and I've never got round to them. And I don't know why.'

Why? It may be that 'putting it off' was modelled by parents or that the brain is muddled by too many tasks or that there is fear of starting something

35

which will end in failure. So 'I don't feel like it' and 'Not just now' win the day. For a dream to be realised it needs to be embodied in a clearly defined goal.

o **The goal.** *Without a goal the dream is nothing.* A young man involved in seventeen different forms of sport said, 'I had strength, speed and stamina, but no sense. I spread myself too widely and as a result I was a jack of all sports and a master of none. My dreams of stardom never came true.' To be effective we must be selective.

To be effective we must be selective

MEMO

What is our role in life, as an individual or in family, work, church or community? Let us identify our roles and clarify our goals. There is strong evidence that those who write down their goals, especially in a place where they are easily seen, are more likely to achieve them. It has been wisely said, 'Don't just think it – ink it.'

A goal is more than a desire; it is a desire over which we have control. We give it priority and devote time and energy to it. Love may not be too strong a word. A goal is what we choose to do or be, and that affects of course what we choose not to do or not to be. We cannot afford to be vague about values whether they are material, emotional, intellectual or spiritual. Without a goal the dream is nothing.

o **The plan.** *Without a plan the goal is nothing.* Inspiration needs organisation. The plan we make is a framework strong enough to bear the weight of our aims, but flexible enough to cope with the unexpected (which always happens). The plan itself does not rule: it is the servant of the goal. If the plan does not work as we had hoped, we revise or replace it. Plans should be firm but flexible.

We may need help with our plan. US President, Woodrow Wilson, laughed, 'I use not only all the brains I have but all I can borrow.' We need not be ashamed to ask for help, at home, in business, for the church, with a hobby. It may mean working alongside another person and that can halve the time and double the enjoyment. Without a plan the goal is nothing.

o **The will.** *Without the will the plan is nothing.* In any project, as in life itself, the secret of success is to be consistent in aim and persistent in action. 'If at first you don't succeed, try, try and try again.' Don't let failure stop us; don't let feelings slow us down. If the goal is clear and the plan in place, don't let's wait to feel like it. Just do it!

Martin Luther King's dream of black and white equality in America would have come to nothing if his dream had not become a goal, a goal about which he was passionate. But the goal would never have been realised without the carefully executed plan of non-violent protest and demonstration in which so many took part. But the plan itself would not have worked without the will to see it through whatever the consequences.

Let us dream our dreams, set our goals, make our plans, and then just do it … and go on doing it (see the authors' book *Just Do It*, CWR, 2006). Success and happiness lie not in dreaming but in doing.

MEMO
Success and happiness lie not in dreaming but in doing

NOTES

1. Mark 12:30
2. C.S. Lewis, *Surprised by Joy.*
3. Stephen Covey, *7 Habits of Highly Effective People.*
4. Romans 12:2
5. Philippians 3:13
6. Philippians 1:21
7. 2 Timothy 4:7
8. Matthew 11:30, *The Message*

Dealing with feelings

¹2m

meaning of love; managing anger; win over worry; shadow of sadness

Dealing with feelings

In looking at our lives we began with the mind because how we think largely determines how we feel. Feelings are such an important part of being human that there are hundreds of words in English that express them.

- **Feelings are individual.** What causes one person to laugh makes another cry, because how they think affects how they feel. One is delighted at the result of the game, another disappointed. Not only do people feel differently, they also express those feelings in different ways. They may be influenced by the way their parents modelled respect, or how they themselves learned unselfishness, or the manner in which affection was expressed in their culture. What leaves one person overwhelmed pushes another to be controlling.

- **Feelings are complex.** A man is killed in a road accident. His wife thinks about what has happened. She is overcome with *grief* over the death of her husband. *Anger* burns against the drunken driver who caused the crash. She is filled with *fear* as to how she will provide for the future, and with *love* for the husband she has lost and the children who will be without a father.

- **Feelings are powerful.** The love of a man for a woman, the love of a parent for a child, whether it is in tundra, jungle, desert or urban sprawl, 'makes the world go round'. And bitterness? Minds are torn apart, families divide, communities are savaged, nations go to war. Love builds, bitterness destroys.

- **Feelings are physical.** Feelings, especially if they are strong, can produce actual physical changes in us. Widely differing emotions like love, fear and anger can have exactly the same effects – rapid breathing, increased heartbeat, muscle tension and sweat.

Of the many human emotions, four of the most common are love, anger, anxiety and sadness – all of which impact a person's happiness.

Meaning of love

LOVE HAS MANY MEANINGS. One of the most used words in the language, love applies both to 'things' and people.

Things. It can range from 'I love chocolate' to a passion for music, sport, work or love of country.

People. The words 'I love you' may express the tenderness of romantic love. They could have the sexual meaning of 'I want you', which might be the voice of enduring commitment or merely lust in love's clothing. They fall from the lips of both parent and child. The words 'I love you, Lord' can be the language of worship and devotion, or hymns sung without heart or meaning.

- **'Love at first sight.'** Love is the recurring theme of songs around the world, some moving and some ridiculous, none more so than the old song which carried the line, 'Hello, I love you, won't you tell me your name?' There can of course be admiration at first sight or sexual attraction, but neither of these is love. Probably the only true 'love at first sight' is when parents gaze at their newborn baby. But even then, behind that first sight there are the months of expectation and often years of love which the parents have shared.

- **'Falling in love.'** The words 'I fell in love' are well understood, and for most people describe the moment or process when love began. Everyone's experience is different. One person described it as, 'not a falling which I couldn't help, but a melting which I thoroughly enjoyed!' 'Falling in love' can be a way of abdicating responsibility ('I couldn't help myself'), and can be used to justify unfaithfulness, desertion and the break up of the family. Love can be strong and wrong at the same time.

- **What is love?** Love is other-centred. The fact that it is more about how we act than how we feel, means we can choose to show love to those we may not naturally like. Indeed, the Bible tells us to love our enemies. Dictionary definitions are hopelessly inadequate, but there is one description that has never been surpassed. In hundreds of languages it has circled the world: 'Love is patient, love is kind. It does not envy, it does not boast, it is not proud. It is not rude, it is not self-seeking, it is not easily angered, it keeps no record of wrongs. Love does not delight in evil but rejoices with the truth. It always protects, always trusts, always hopes, always perseveres. Love never fails.'[1] These biblical words show that love is active not passive. It is defined not by *feeling* but by *doing* and by what it chooses *not to do.*

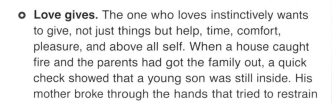

MEMO

'Love ... keeps no record of wrongs'

- **Love gives.** The one who loves instinctively wants to give, not just things but help, time, comfort, pleasure, and above all self. When a house caught fire and the parents had got the family out, a quick check showed that a young son was still inside. His mother broke through the hands that tried to restrain her and rushed into the burning building. When the firemen finally put out the flames, the mother's body was found on the bedroom floor with her hands outstretched to the bed where her son lay. Love gives everything; even life itself.

o **Love grows.** The emotional high of infatuation never lasts (though tell that to the infatuated!). Plants and people grow at different rates, sometimes slowly, at times in spurts. Love is the same. There are even times when it seems to grow downwards! How many bewildered parents have said of their young people, 'I know I love them, but right at this moment I don't even *like* them!' Love is tested by the times we can't feel it.

> ## Love is tested by the times we can't feel it
>
> MEMO

o **Love can be lost.** Love can be dulled by routine, scarred by abuse or lost by silence and neglect. It can wither and die. As a plant needs water, love needs nurture. The principle is the same for love between friends, parents and children, wives and husbands. Love can reach heights – and depths.

o **Love can be recaptured.** A husband sat with a counsellor and said, 'I have lost my love for my wife.' Counsellor and client established that the man had allowed business to overwhelm their marriage, until communication was reduced to a few mutterings in front of the TV. Then silence in the sitting room became silence in the bedroom. The man said that if there was one word which described their relationship it was 'nothingness'.

The counsellor replied, 'The love you say you have lost is a *noun*, but you can still choose to love, for love is also a *verb*. There is something you can do. You can choose to go out together as you used to, you can choose to talk, choose to be thoughtful, choose little kindnesses, yes, choose touch. What you *do* affects how you *feel*.' When the husband began hesitantly to reach out to his wife, she equally hesitantly began to respond. Slowly at first, and then with gathering momentum, love grew until the noun was recaptured by the verb. They said later, 'We deserved to be unhappy because we did nothing to keep our love alive', and later still they added, 'The more we *do* the more we *feel*.'

MEMO

'Love is … a verb'

Managing anger

Red-faced and loud-voiced anger is matched by a frosty face and silent sulk. 'Angry? Of course I'm not angry' – which interpreted is, 'I'm mad at you, but won't admit it!'

Is anger always wrong? No, in itself it is neither good nor bad, but a normal reaction to threat, hurt or frustration. Anger at social injustice drove forward the campaigns to abolish slavery, create trade unions and get votes for women, and the New Testament shows a Jesus angry with the hypocrisy of the Pharisees. Anger can be right, but mostly it's negative and damaging, with only one letter (d) away from 'danger'. So, what lies behind it and how do we deal with it?

MEMO

Anger … only one letter … away from 'danger'

UNDERSTANDING IT. Some people by temperament are more uptight than others, though that does not excuse lack of control. It is good if possible to find the cause of our anger by completing the sentence – 'I am angry because …' If the cause is difficult to identify, it may even be rooted in early years. A woman was angry that she did not receive a birthday card she had been expecting. Many would see that as trivial, but for her, with years of childhood rejection behind her, the-card-that-didn't-come dipped into a pool of pain from the-love-which-wasn't-given. Understanding ourselves is halfway to understanding our anger.

EXPRESSING IT. Some say it's best to 'let it out'. If by that is meant venting rage and tearing strips off people, then no, it's worst, not best, for both parties. Misery can be inflicted by anger whether it is expressed violently, verbally or by sullen silence. And, of course, angry people hurt themselves.

It is said that in ancient Greece there were two athletes, one of whom was honoured by the city fathers with a statue. His rival was consumed with anger that showed itself in the nightly attack he made on the statue. Eventually he succeeded in knocking it down. And it fell on him – and killed him! Angry people are more likely to have heart and other conditions, and more than one doctor has said they felt that anger was the real 'cause of death'.

If we feel angry it can be good to talk it over with someone we trust. We might find a different perspective. However 'letting it out' *at* the person against whom we are angry is another matter. But if it is important to explain to that person how we think and feel, possibly to prevent bigger problems later, then *how we do it* is crucial. In dealing with an issue, we should aim to use words that deal with the problem but preserve the relationship.

MEMO

... deal with the problem but preserve the relationship

SUPPRESSING IT. It's not good to 'bottle it up'. We can stuff it down so firmly that we come to think that we are not angry at all. But our anger doesn't go away. It lurks in the subconscious and may spread into other areas of our lives. Anger can be the root of depression and at the back of addiction.

PREVENTING IT. Prevention is better than cure and if we can identify the things which trigger our anger we can often avoid the problems. Above all, we should guard our time, for if we are overcommitted we will be overtired, and if we are overtired it is much easier to 'lose it'.

CONTROLLING IT

o **Press the pause button.** If we feel tension beginning to rise inside us, let's press the pause button in our mind – *stop and think*. A four-hour argument between a husband and wife began with conflict over whether the toilet roll should curl inwards or outwards, and (as both testified) almost ended in suicide. We should ask, 'Is it worth it?' before we get to the place where we know it isn't.

o **Use 'First Aid'.** That's something which helps us relax. We breathe slowly, making our out-breath slower than the in-breath, drink a cup of tea, sing (it's hard to sing and be angry at the same time), reach for a book or magazine, do something we enjoy. Or simply do what Thomas Jefferson famously recommended: 'When angry, count to ten before you speak. If very angry, count to one hundred.'

> ## 'When angry, count to ten before you speak. If very angry, count to one hundred'
> **MEMO**

- **Speak calmly.** If two people interrupt each other then the voices become louder and louder. And, of course, anger climbs with raised voices. We can be quiet but firm, and firm but courteous. The Bible reminds us that, 'A gentle response defuses anger …'[2] It does, the anger of both speaker and spoken to.

- **Choose our words**
  Don't exaggerate. When we exaggerate someone's fault, we unconsciously justify to ourselves our anger, and make it worse. And, of course, the person on the receiving end of our exaggeration becomes angry because they know what we said is not fair.
  Accept responsibility for our anger. We should not say, 'You make me so angry'. There may have been words or actions that have been careless and hurtful, but in the end it is our reaction which determines whether or not we become angry. It is much better to say, 'I feel angry because …' and give our reasons. And we should neither use force nor threaten it.

- **Do good … say good … feel good.** C.S. Lewis wrote, 'If you injure someone you dislike, you will find yourself disliking him more. If you do him a good turn, you will find yourself disliking him less.'[3] What we do and what we say affect how we feel.

- **Letting it go.** A man felt he had been unfairly treated by the company to which he had given long and loyal service. He was angry without knowing it. Wakeful nights, words echoing from the past, a pain in the chest that drove him to the doctor, brought him to see that he was creating his own bitterness. Speaking of it afterwards he said, 'One day I let it go. Almost immediately there was release. The fight with myself was over, and I walked free.'

In one sense, whether we are right or wrong doesn't matter; the more we rehearse what happened, the angrier we get. So let's not dwell on it. We can't alter the past, only our attitude to it. If there is something that is still unresolved, we can bury the hatchet if not the issue. Many have used the prayer, 'God grant me the serenity to accept the things I cannot change, courage to change the things I can, and the wisdom to know the difference.'

MEMO

We can bury the hatchet if not the issue

USING IT. Behind campaigns like Make Poverty History and Stop the Traffik has been outrage at injustice. On a personal level it can strengthen our resolve to get things done, for anger gives courage to deal with issues. Then as we use it, we defuse it, and it works *for* us, not *against* us.

Win over worry

Anxiety is part of being human and is not necessarily bad. It can push the student faced with an exam to work harder, motivate the athlete to train or challenge a parent to spend more time with the children. A degree of nervousness is felt by everyone sometimes. But anxiety is usually experienced negatively as a response to a threat, imagined or real. The subject is a large and complex one, so we will focus on worry, its most common form.

'STEWING WITHOUT DOING.' Concern about work or health or family is natural and can lead to action with good outcomes. But worry is unbalanced concern. Concern has wholesome routines, worry has ruts. It has been called 'stewing without doing'. It's a road with no exit and no end because it always comes back to where it began. Repetition reinforces remembered hurts and converts difficulties into seeming catastrophes. It rarely comes up with new solutions, but leaves the worrier confused, depressed and even ill.

> # Worry is 'stewing without doing'
>
> **MEMO**

There can be physical symptoms, such as headaches, nausea, sweating, trembling, a pounding heart or over-activity of the intestines. These are caused by the increase of adrenalin in the blood. They are short-term and unpleasant, but long-term anxiety can lead to fears and phobias that need professional expertise. We can literally become 'worried sick'.

The word 'worry' comes from an Old English word meaning 'to strangle'. And that's what it does. It puts a stranglehold on us; wastes our time, dissipates our energy, encourages procrastination and can paralyse us into inactivity. It affects concentration, knocks confidence, disturbs sleep and leaves us exhausted. It is not only useless but worse than useless. It is said that, 'Worry doesn't empty tomorrow of its sorrow, it empties today of its strength'.

We need more than a kindly meant 'Don't worry!' We need a plan. Here's one that is road-tested.

HAVING A PLAN

o **Checking the problem.** Is it *something*, an event we fear; or *somewhere*, a place or situation with bad associations; or *someone* we are not sure we can cope with? What triggers it? By establishing the 'think-link' with worry we may stop it from starting!

MEMO

Establish the 'think-link' with worry

○ **Challenging worries.** Ask, 'Is there another way of looking at this? Is it the situation that needs changing or my attitude? Could I be more flexible? Have I got it out of proportion?

○ **Avoiding the situation.** Money worries are some of the biggest and blackest, for debt is so easy to get into and so hard to get out of. Someone joked, 'If your outgoings exceed your income then your upkeep will be your downfall.' There is, of course, a turn of events we could not have predicted, but problems can often be avoided by careful planning. Budgeting, which many find hard, is better than worrying.

○ **Talking it over.** To talk it over with a person whose judgment we trust can prove to be a major step forward. We might get good advice, or even find the problem we thought was a mountain is only a molehill. But *to go on talking* about it is counterproductive, because the more we talk about it the more we'll think about it, and the more we think about it the more we'll worry.

○ **Reminding ourselves.** Jesus showed the waste of worry by asking, 'Who of you by worrying can add a single hour to his life?'[4] The answer of course is no one. If we are concerned about what course of action to take, it is good to remind ourselves that God is as keen (and more so) that we should know his will as we are to find it. And those who trust him are at peace because they are assured that 'absolutely *nothing* can get between us and God's love …'[5] And we are reminded, 'Don't fret or worry. Instead of worrying, pray. Let petitions and praises shape your worries into prayers, letting God know your concerns.'[6]

- **Catching it early.** When worry jumps into our mind (again), let's slam the door in its face and say, 'No way! Get lost!' The quicker we do it the easier it is.

- **Relaxing ourselves.** If we have found relaxation techniques helpful (deep breathing and the tensing and relaxing of muscles) then now is the time to use them. Quite apart from the benefit of relaxing, in thinking about the exercises we switch off from the worry.

- **Getting on with it.** The more we put off doing what we know we should do, the more we worry. 'It' hangs there in our mind. The best way to banish worry is to get the job done!

- **Facing it squarely.** A woman, after a difficult birth, suffered from agoraphobia and became fearful of flying. But she did not give in. At first flying with her husband, 'Digging,' he said, 'her fingernails into the palm of my hand'; then more calmly with him; later nervously without him; then flying on her own without a care in the world. She faced it, fought it and overcame it.

Shadow of sadness

She asked, 'How are you?' and he answered, 'Fine!' But he wasn't. If there was one word which described him it would be 'disappointed'. He felt let down by one to whom he had looked up. There were memories he did not want to remember. He could not talk about these things and hid his hurt with laughter.

His sadness was private, but often sorrow is very public. Death has brought the loss of a loved one; unemployment has reared its ugly head; illness or accident has meant undreamed-of limitations; divorce has torn a family apart.

Whether the feeling of being sad passes quickly or is deep and long lasting, it is the experience of *everyone*. There are *no* exceptions. We cannot wave a hand and banish sorrow from life for it is a natural human emotion. Psychologist Carl Jung said, 'There are as many nights as days … and even a happy life cannot be without a measure of darkness, and the word "happy" would lose its meaning if it were not balanced by sadness.'

o **Be careful of 'why?'** It is natural to ask 'Why?' or 'Why me?', and if we find an answer, fine. But if no answer comes, then it is unwise to pursue it endlessly, for doing so only keeps the pain alive. It's best to say, 'It happened; I don't understand it, but I'll get on with living.' Amy Carmichael spent much of her life rescuing and caring for neglected children in India. Injured in a fall she was hardly outside her bedroom for seventeen years, but found, she said, 'in acceptance there is liberty'.

MEMO

'In acceptance there is liberty'

o **It's OK to cry.** 'Big boys don't cry' is nonsense, and dangerous nonsense at that. Crying is a natural expression of sadness and is often part of recovery. Not all sorrow needs to be escaped; some needs to be lived through. Especially where there is the loss of a loved one, it is good to grieve, and for that time is needed. For lost love there is no quick healing.

○ **Talking it over.** If we are sad then it can help to talk with someone who listens not just to the facts but to our feelings. A person who is seriously depressed will need professional help, but mostly sorrow just needs an ear to listen and a shoulder to cry on. Sadness needs understanding more than advice.

Sadness needs understanding more than advice

MEMO

○ **Watch out for wallowing.** We may have good reason to be sad but we must watch out for wallowing. In facing the facts we should not distort them, and must guard against generalising with 'Nobody cares' or 'There I go again'. When we count our blessings, the good things and people in our life, we may be surprised how much there is to be grateful for. The glass is, after all, half full and not half empty.

○ **Don't stay in the past.** Small sorrows slip from the memory as if they had never happened; big ones don't, especially where there have been major hurts. But we can control how often we visit our memory, and refuse to let the past destroy the present.

○ **Sensibly busy.** A life which has purpose and meaning, rewarding work and warm relationships, fulfilling interests and physical activity, will deal more easily with sorrow when it comes. Sadness is helped by being sensibly busy.

○ **Upwards and outwards.** Joni Eareckson Tada, the girl paralysed in all four limbs after her diving accident, was happy, not because of her handicap but in spite of it. Joni came to a place in her life when she was able to say, 'God, if I can't die, please show me how to live.'

Slowly, she said, there came 'a warm, deep, personal relationship with Jesus', and she could pray mischievously, 'God, you have the strength. You have the resources. Can I please borrow your smile?' She began to reach out to others, and today, Joni and Friends, the organisation she founded, makes wheelchairs available to paralysed people in more than half the countries of the world. Her happiness lies in looking not backwards or downwards but outwards and upwards.

NOTES

1. 1 Corinthians 13:4–8
2. Proverbs 15:1, *The Message*
3. C.S. Lewis, *Mere Christianity.*
4. Matthew 6:27
5. Romans 8:39, *The Message*
6. Philippians 4:6, *The Message*

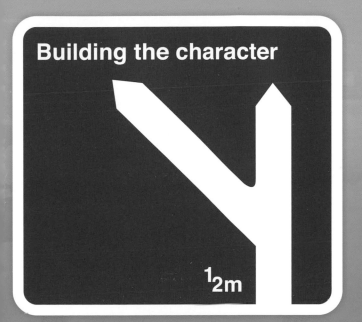

Building the character

$\frac{1}{2}$m

humility – opens the door;
integrity – sticking by values;
forgiveness and freedom;
habits – making and breaking

How we manage our mind and deal with our feelings powerfully influences the character we develop. Then, for better or for worse, from character comes conduct. These two are so closely linked that behaviour which is typical of a person is said to be 'characteristic', while that which is not typical is 'out of character'. What we do, we become; what we are, we do.

MEMO

What we do, we become; what we are, we do

'All my life,' a student admitted, 'I have blamed my father for what I am, but now I realise that I am responsible for me.' Well said! Children are greatly influenced by parents, and teenagers by friends, but in the end, character is a choice. Consciously or unconsciously we are the sum of our habits. The Greek philosopher, Aristotle, rightly taught, 'We are what we repeatedly do.' Character is the core or 'stuff' of which we are made, and is shown not by a single word or act but by our way of life. How we react to the unexpected depends almost entirely on how we normally act.

The building blocks of good character start with *humility* which opens the door to truth and relationship, *integrity* which sticks by values whatever the cost, and *forgiveness* without which there is no freedom. That means, of course, there are *habits* – some to be broken, others to be made.

Humility – opens the door

PRIDE AND PREJUDICE. Pride is ugly when we see it in someone else, but it is like bad breath; the person who has it is the last to know it! Where does pride come from?

o **Ignorance.** You cannot tell anything to the know-all; they have been there, done that. 'Looking back,' said one, 'I am embarrassed by my ignorance. I simply did not *know* that there was another (and better) way of looking at things. The assumption that I was completely right can be summed up in one word – prejudice.'

o **Insecurity.** Much boasting is rooted in insecurity. Desperately unsure of himself, a man tried to prove that he was superior by criticising everyone else. But, of course, when he pointed his finger, three fingers pointed back at him.

o **Success.** For her, success was not enough. Success was not success unless everyone knew it. When they looked up to her, she could then look down on them, and she liked that.

What do the proud find? They find they have built a wall. True, the proud will have 'friends' who want to share their success or fame or money, but often there is no depth to the friendship because there is no warmth in pride. Then, of course, 'Pride goes ... before a fall'.[1]

'Pride goes ... before a fall'

MEMO

HUMILITY IS HONESTY. Humility is fundamental to strength of character. It is not timidity or weakness, nor is it the hypocrisy of Uriah Heep, in Dickens' novel *David Copperfield*, whose 'I am ever so 'umble' was a screen for ambition and greed. Rather, humility is the honesty that does not pretend to be better or greater. It is not thinking less of ourselves but thinking of ourselves less. Humble people are able to acknowledge success but do not boast of it; they accept praise but reject flattery. But where does humility come from? It may come as a surprise but the Bible says, 'Humble yourselves ...',[2] so it is something *we do*. What and how?

o **Confessing wrong**. When the proud say, 'I am wrong', they are on their way to being right! If there has been hurt or harm, then 'I am sorry' needs to follow 'I am wrong', remembering that an apology is a sign of strength, not weakness. Never spoil an apology with an excuse.

o **Admitting ignorance.** There is nothing demeaning in answering a question with a frank, 'I don't know', or receiving information with interest and thanks. Some of the greatest minds have been the most humble, and it was their admission of ignorance that led to their search for truth. Humility is the door to learning.

MEMO

Humility is the door to learning

o **Accepting criticism.** Often criticism is neither all right nor all wrong but a mixture of true and false. The humble will look for an element of truth even in the harshest criticism. One person said, 'I thank God for my critics. The greatest lessons of my life I learned through them.'

- **Sharing success.** If we have been successful, whenever possible let's share our success with others. If they contributed to the success, we acknowledge it frankly with, 'She played a part in this' or 'I couldn't have done it without him.'

- **Being courteous.** Being humble does not mean that we have no firm opinions or that we allow people to walk all over us. But it does mean being courteous, and treating people with dignity even if they don't deserve it. If a prediction of ours turns out to be right, let's be careful of saying, 'I told you so!'

- **Giving praise.** If we are glad when others fail and resent it when they succeed, let's try what one person found. 'Whenever I find myself thinking negatively about anyone, I deliberately take every opportunity to speak well of them. I find that if I *speak* positively about them it helps me to *think* positively about them also. My thoughts change my words, and my words change my thoughts!'

'... thoughts change words, and ... words change thoughts!'

MEMO

- **Choosing to pray.** The proud humble themselves by the very act of prayer, for prayer says, 'I need help'.

- **Following the example of Jesus.** There is no better example of humility than Jesus. It was not beneath his dignity to take a towel and basin of water and wash twelve pairs of dirty feet. He served those he led.

The effect of humility is twofold. Horizontally, it opens the door to closer relationships with people. Anger comes more slowly, honesty more readily, harmony more easily. Vertically, it opens the door to God's grace.

Jesus told the parable of two men praying. The first said, 'God, I thank you that I am not like other men …' and listed his credits. The second prayed simply, 'God, have mercy on me, a sinner.' The one was saying, 'Accept me because I am so good', the other, 'Accept me although I'm so bad'. Jesus said of the latter, 'I tell you that this man, rather than the other, went home justified before God. For everyone who exalts himself will be humbled, and he who humbles himself will be exalted'.[3]

Integrity – sticking by values

A driver of supply trucks for Coca-Cola used to drink cans of Pepsi while at work. He may have preferred the taste or thought it funny, but the management thought otherwise. They reckoned the company was undermined by his actions. The principle is the same for everyone everywhere; let actions match values. A life of integrity is fundamental to character.

COURAGE. Heroism is generally thought of as a supreme act of bravery: a soldier in battle or the rescue of a drowning person. But to stand daily for what is right against the thinking or behaviour of those around also requires courage. Courage is not so much an absence of fear as the willingness to act in spite of it.

TRUTH. The President of the world's most powerful country had to resign because he lied. It was the 'whitewash at the White House' when integrity was sacrificed for expediency. Top politicians in the UK have ended in gaol, not because of what they did, but because they lied in court. There's wisdom in the saying, 'Truth fears no questions'.

'Truth fears no questions'

MEMO

'Tell him I'm out,' said the boss. The receptionist explained to the enquirer that he was not available, and later told her boss what she had done. He was furious that she had not followed his instructions. She replied quietly, 'I am employed to work, not to lie.' Then she added, 'Besides, if I were to lie *for* you, you would not know whether I might lie *to* you.' There is wisdom as well as humour in Mark Twain's reminder, 'If you tell the truth you will not need a good memory!'

MONEY. A small boy came home from a corner shop with a bar of chocolate. His mother knew he didn't have the money in his pocket and asked how he got it. He said, 'The woman gave it to me.' She hauled him back to the shop, wriggling with embarrassment; made him apologise to the shopkeeper and pay for the chocolate. Years later, trusted by government and decorated by the Queen, a leader of several organisations, he said, 'I will never forget that moment in the shop. It marked my life forever.'

WORK. A casual and careless attitude to work that wasted a company's time, and therefore frustrated its management and impacted its finances, apparently caused the head of one New York firm to post the following on the notice board. 'Some time between starting and quitting time, without infringing on lunch periods, coffee breaks, rest periods, storytelling, ticket selling, holiday planning, and the rehashing of yesterday's television programmes, we ask that each employee try to find some time for a work break. This may seem radical, but it might aid steady employment and assure regular pay cheques.'

Where there is integrity there is trust. We are trusted with time when it is known we will do a good day's work, with money for it will never stick to our hands, with colleagues for we will treat them well, with a particular job for we will do it thoroughly, and with the company's reputation which we take seriously. There will be no inflated expense accounts, no misuse of computers and no 'sickies' which are not genuine. We choose integrity and earn trust.

MEMO

... choose integrity and earn trust

PROMISES. Do they say of us, 'If she says it, she'll do it' or 'If he promises he'll have it by Friday, he'll have it by Friday'? Whether it is task or time, we deliver.

Promises are meant to be kept, but sometimes integrity demands they be broken.

'Oh, but you promised!' has pressured people into drugs or sex, when common sense should have answered, 'Sorry, I shouldn't have made that promise, and the answer is "No."' Or totally unforeseen circumstances might arise when we have to say, 'I didn't realise the implications of what I had taken on, and I'm sorry to disappoint you.'

But mostly a promise is a promise. At the end of a long day a tired parent doesn't feel like playing, as promised, with the children, but does it anyway. A commitment made in church or work or club is carried out. In every area of life dependability is highly prized, and in none more highly than in marriage when the vows of loyalty made to each other are faithfully kept.

CONSISTENCY. The harshest criticism of Jesus was reserved for the Pharisees and their lack of integrity, and forever 'hypocrite' (from a Greek word for actor) is linked with them. They were super-religious on the outside, yet on the inside they were 'maggoty with greed and secret evil'.[4]

The higher we aim the more we will be watched

by those who hope we will succeed and (let us be warned) by some who will want us to fail. So let's walk our talk, and make sure our standards are 'exactly what it says on the tin'!

Forgiveness and freedom

FORGIVENESS IS A CHOICE. 'I can never forgive him,' she said, as if she couldn't help it. But she was wrong. Just as we choose to be unselfish when the opposite is more attractive, so forgiveness is more choice than feeling. How do we deal with hurt?

o **Choose not to dwell on it.** It's often said, 'You can't help birds flying over your head, but you can stop them nesting in your hair.' We can't help that unwelcome thought which arrives out of nowhere. In a fraction of a moment it's there, wounding and unwanted. But we are responsible if we let it stay there. We can say 'no', and switch our mind to something else. Difficult at first, the 'no and switch' gradually becomes a habit until, as one person put it, 'There was hardly a day I didn't think about it, now there's hardly a day I do.'

o **Choose not to talk about it.** If we talk about anything, we think about it (we can't do otherwise). If we think about it, we feel it (we can't do otherwise). So that's how it works if we talk about something which was hurtful. Talk … think … feel … pain. Who caused our pain just now? We did! That painful thing could have been years ago, but by talking about it we have just brought it back to life.

o **Choose not to retaliate.** Feelings may say, 'You did it to me, I'll do it to you'; forgiveness says, 'I could but I won't.' What better example is there than that of Jesus who, 'When they hurled their insults at him … did not retaliate …'[5]

o **Choose to let it go.** A man wrote down every bad thing (as he saw it) that his wife had done to him over a period of twenty years. Nobody knew anything about it – until his wife found the list! Because he kept looking back he could not move forward, either in life or marriage. Mahatma Gandhi said, 'The weak can never forgive. Forgiveness is the attribute of the strong.'

FORGIVENESS SETS US FREE

o **God's forgiveness.** The greatest incentive for forgiving others is our own forgiveness by God. One person described their experience of forgiveness by saying it was as if, 'God had got a great big scrubbing brush and scrubbed me clean inside'. Another said, 'If God has set *me* free, how can I leave anyone else in prison?'

o **Harmony.** Gripes, grudges and grunts, by outburst, withdrawal or silence, lock us into the past. Bitterness is a barrier to relationship; forgiveness a door to new beginning.

MEMO

**Bitterness is a barrier …
forgiveness a door …**

o **Peace of mind.** The world stood amazed when Nelson Mandela emerged without bitterness from twenty-seven years in prison. His explanation was simple, 'If you hate, you will give them your heart and mind. Don't give those two things away.' We have a choice – we forgive or fester.

o **Good health.** Every doctor has patients whose conditions are made worse, or even caused, by gnawing resentment. Broken sleep, headaches, chest pains, ulcers, depression and breakdown are among them. In some cases forgiveness may even make medicine unnecessary and healing more lasting.

THE HOW OF FORGIVING

o **From the heart.** If someone comes to us and asks, 'Will you forgive me?' he is wanting to hear the words, 'Yes, I do.' But if we go and say, 'I forgive you', he may well reply 'For what?' Nine times out of ten he will not think he has done anything wrong. Forgiveness doesn't always have to be on the lips if it's there in the heart.

o **Avoid the blame game.** Check if we have contributed to the problem. Jesus asked, 'Why do you look at the speck of sawdust in your brother's eye and pay no attention to the plank in your own eye?'[6] Perhaps we need forgiveness as much as others do.

o **Go easy on them.** Let's avoid the temptation of making others look bad by talking about what they did wrong or how they hurt us. Forgiveness is silent about the faults of others.

Forgiveness is silent about the faults of others

MEMO

o **As soon as possible.** If the offence is small, and especially if it was not deliberate, then the forgiveness may be immediate. But what if the hurt is big, and particularly if it comes from something ongoing and deliberate? Well, if the person admits the offence, that makes it easier; if the person gives up doing that wrong, it makes it easier still. But supposing there is no apology and no change – say ongoing violence or adultery – then forgiveness may take time; possibly a very long time. But even if there is no change, if we forgive, then in the end we walk free.

FORGIVENESS AND RECONCILIATION. Does forgiveness mean reconciliation?

o **Sometimes 'yes'.** In the story of the Prodigal Son, forgiveness and reconciliation were wrapped together in the same hug. We hear it in the moving words, '… this son of mine was dead and is alive again; he was lost and is found.' [7]

o **Sometimes 'no'.** A girl, sexually abused by her father, grew to womanhood, marriage and motherhood. Bitterness gnawed at her heart for years until one day she wrote to her father. She said, 'I told him how my life had been ruined by what he had done to me, and went on to tell him that I forgave him. I remember the sense of release that swept over me as I heard the sound of my letter falling to the bottom of the postbox.' But she never allowed her father to have contact with her children. What he had done to her, he might do to them, and she could not risk it. Reconciliation was not possible, for though she had forgiven she dared not trust.

Habits – making and breaking

A habit is something we routinely do with little or no conscious decision. In itself it is neither good nor bad. A bad habit is one which hinders or harms us or other people, or is intrinsically wrong; a good habit benefits us or others, or is intrinsically right.

The roots of habit often lie in childhood, even before memory begins, but all adults are responsible for their habits. We form our habits, good or bad, and then, of course, they form us. There are no instant habits. They are the result of our choices, even the choice of doing nothing to change them!

THE BAD AND THE GOOD

Identify the habit. Know our enemy! Is it overeating, overspending, losing our temper, smoking, drinking too much or just plain selfishness? It may be tough to admit to a bad habit, but we can't change what we don't admit.

> ### … we can't change what we don't admit

MEMO

- **Examine the reasons.** A bad habit gives instant gratification. We gain pleasure (the pleasure of binging, tearing strips off someone, eating ten bags of crisps a day) or we avoid pain (the pain of writing tedious letters or taking much needed exercise). In some form, pleasure and pain are the main reasons for bad habits.

- **Consider the consequences.** Are our habits frankly unhealthy, a waste of time and talent, and do they hurt or antagonise people? If so, then if we break them we will have more time, better health and relationships and a fuller life with more energy to enjoy it. Breaking one bad habit helps us break others, just as making one good habit helps us make more. The effects of habits are cumulative.

- **Choose a strategy.** When we were learning to drive, the car jerked and jumped and we wondered if we would ever master it. But we did. Now we can listen to the radio, talk with a passenger, keep our eye on the road, and at the same time make complex manoeuvres almost without thinking. Driving is a habit. How did we learn? By repetition. We did the same things over and over again until we were hardly conscious of doing them. That's how we make or break habits. Here's a strategy –

Setting our sights. Let's be clear about what we are aiming to change, and then make a plan that fits the purpose.

Having a clear motive. A primary school principal told the parents of one of the children, 'Your son is not happy. He's constantly crying.' Their probing brought her reply, 'Well, frankly, it's because you smoke.' 'What's that got to do with it?' The answer came, 'Your son has learned that "Smoking kills". He's convinced you are both going to die.' The parents, both of whom were heavy smokers, never smoked again. Their motivation broke their habit.

Getting support. There may be things of a private nature that are difficult or unwise for us to share, but if possible we should 'go public'. It's harder to fall back into old ways if we have told others what we are doing. Their encouragement will help our progress. We may even get into a shared routine with others that benefits both them and us.

Talking to ourselves. Henry Ford, an immensely successful man, grinned, 'Whether you think that you can, or think that you can't, you are usually right!' It helps to talk to ourselves and to say, 'Yes, I *can* do it.' And to *talk back* to the bad habit, giving 'it' a name and saying, 'Get lost. I have better things to do.'

Seeing success. Let's begin with what we want the outcome to be. Have we a habit of saying 'yes' to everything we are asked to do? Then let us see ourselves saying 'no' politely but firmly. We can practise in front of a mirror. 'I'm sorry; some other time maybe. Right now I am fully committed.' Imagination has been called the workshop of the mind and increasingly we will do what we see. Seeing success can break the cycle of failure.

Praying. Say the problem is overeating. We pray about it, not dwelling on the food but the person that with God's help we want to be. Then when temptation comes, we lift our heart in prayer and throw the goodies out! We might even call that 'faith and works'.

Seeing success can break the cycle of failure

MEMO

Practising control. We may say 'no' (sometimes) to feelings, even if they are perfectly legitimate. 'I'm still hungry but today I'll skip the dessert.' 'I'm thirsty but I'll take a glass of water rather than coffee.' 'I'm tired but I'll go for a walk.' There is nothing wrong with hunger, thirst or tiredness, but our firm 'no' when it is not vital strengthens our will for a bigger 'no' when it will be.

Celebrating. When it comes to habits, carrots are better than sticks. We can tell ourselves, 'When we have done *this* we will have the pleasure of *that*.' Rather than punishing ourselves for failing, we reward ourselves for succeeding. Celebrate!

... carrots are better than sticks

MEMO

Carry it through. Habits are not formed in a day or changed in a day. A cigarette manufacturer used to advertise, 'Take our 30-day test'. No wonder; they guessed if they got someone for a month, they had got them. Are we breaking an old habit or making a new one? If we do it for thirty days it's a good start, and it's possible we may have it for life. 'Repetition is the mother of success.'

If (or when) we slip up, we don't give up. When we were learning to walk and we fell down, we didn't lie there and cry, 'I'm giving up walking as a bad job.' We got up and went on. The rule is never give up. Bad habits broken and good habits made spell freedom, and even though we weren't looking for it, that brings happiness.

CHARACTER DOESN'T STAY STILL

Everyone grows older but not everyone grows up. Character can go both ways. Some people end up as bundles of complaint and grievance, miserable themselves and spreading their misery around. Others, even in the face of adversity or the teeth of opposition, never stop growing. What the Bible says is true of them, '... suffering produces perseverance; perseverance, character; and character, hope'.[8]

NOTES

1. Proverbs 16:18
2. 1 Peter 5:6
3. Luke 18:10–14
4. Luke 11:39, *The Message*
5. 1 Peter 2:23
6. Matthew 7:3
7. Luke 15:24
8. Romans 5:3–4

Growing in spirit

^{1}2m

facts of faith; undivided heart;
called to serve; under attack

Growing in spirit

Thinking, feeling and choosing combine to make character, and that is true for everyone. It is part of being human. But there is another dimension, the spiritual, which is not simply an 'add-on' to life, like a hobby we happen to be drawn to or an optional extra if we feel inclined. It is so fundamental that Jesus asked, 'What good is it for a man to gain the whole world, yet forfeit his soul? Or what can a man give in exchange for his soul?'[1] The extent to which the spiritual part of our being is alive and growing, greatly affects the people we become. Faith, love and service are central to this.

Facts of faith

A man who had great difficulties with faith explained, 'Even when engulfed by doubt I was captivated by Jesus. I saw kindness in his touching the untouchable, humanness in crying at the death of his friend, dignity in the face of injustice, forgiveness while he was dying. I found his goodness immensely attractive, and even when I didn't fully believe, I wanted to be like him. Now that I do believe, I want that even more.'

BASIS OF FAITH. Lack of growth can come from lack of knowledge. If a person fears that his or her faith may turn out to be 'a firm belief in something for which there is no evidence', there will be neither growth nor happiness. Doubt and joy simply do not go together. But the Christian faith is solidly rooted in history, and for much of the world, time is simply divided into BC and AD, before and after Jesus came.

Former atheist C.S. Lewis wrote that with Jesus,

'there is no half-way house and no parallel in other religions'. His claim to be the Son of God was either true or else he was 'on the level of a man who calls himself a poached egg'. And no one has ever said that.

MEANING OF FAITH. It is one thing to *believe about* Jesus and quite another to *believe in* him. A woman said, 'There were a hundred things I believed about the man who became my husband: height, build, colour of eyes and hair, where he came from, what his job was, his parents, personality, likes and dislikes. But these facts did not make him my husband; my faith did. I believed in him so much I committed myself to him.' She went on, 'It is exactly like that with Jesus. *My faith in him means I am committed to him.*'

It's not *when we were born* that matters but *the fact we are alive*

MEMO

BEGINNINGS OF FAITH. Russian writer, Andrei Bitov, having grown up under atheistic Communism, explains how in his twenty-seventh year, while riding the metro in Leningrad he 'was overcome with a despair so great that life seemed to stop at once, pre-empting the future entirely, let alone any meaning. Suddenly, all by itself, a phrase appeared: *Without God life makes no sense.* Repeating it in astonishment, I rode the phrase up like a moving staircase, got out of the metro and walked into God's light.'

For some there is a place, a day, a time, when faith begins. The apostle Paul's dramatic encounter with Christ on the Damascus road was one such. Others whose faith is just as real recall no date for its beginning. That is not surprising. We would not know the date we were born if we had not been told. It's not *when we were born* that matters but *the fact we are alive*, and those brought up in an atmosphere of faith may have no memory as to how it began.

RENEWING OF FAITH. But what if faith wavers and love grows cold? There may have been disappointment with those who led the way, discouragement from personal failure, or outright rebellion. But whatever the cause, the road back is open. One man, who had turned away from God and lived for years without any spiritual dimension, said simply, 'I chose to return.' Like the prodigal son, he found a father who had never stopped loving and a welcome he could not have believed possible. He who had been to all intents and purposes 'dead' became 'alive again'.[2] His best years were ahead.

ASSURANCE OF FAITH. We cannot be happy if we doubt *the* faith (whether it is true) or *our* faith (whether it is real). Being intellectually or personally sure is not presumptuous. Indeed, with the promise Christ has made to those who follow him – '… I am with you always …'[3] – presumption would not be in believing, but in doubting. His words, not our feelings, are the basis of assurance.

Undivided heart

'With all your heart' – that's where joy lies. If wife and husband make little effort to sustain their marriage, they will be not happy. Half-hearted students disappoint their teachers and lose out themselves. But the reverse is also true. It is the players who are wholly committed who enjoy the game. As with wholeheartedness and happiness, so it is with holiness and happiness. C.S. Lewis was right in admitting, 'We are half-hearted creatures, fooling about with drink and sex and ambition when infinite joy is offered to us.' The biblical command, 'Love the Lord your God with all your heart …'[4] far from being a demand full of menace, is a pathway to joy, for joy lies in an undivided heart.

... joy lies in an undivided heart

MEMO

That does not mean that if we are wholly committed to Christ life has no problems. Commitment *makes* problems! There are things we once accepted as part of life we may now want to resist. We are not promised prosperity or an easy ride. An ambition may have to go, a habit be broken, a friendship lost. Jesus said there will be those who will 'insult you, persecute you and falsely say all kinds of evil against you because of me'. He goes on to say that when this happens we can 'Rejoice and be glad'.[5] Does this mean we will enjoy suffering? Of course not. But this is a happiness that has a deeper dimension, for the suffering is *for his sake* and shows we are loyal to him. We can have joy without enjoyment!

We can have joy without enjoyment!

MEMO

Charles Colson, close confidant of President Nixon, went from the White House to prison. He said, 'I had spent my first 40 years seeking the whole world, to the neglect of my soul. But what I couldn't find in my quest for power and success – that is, true meaning and security – I discovered in prison, where all worldly props had been stripped away. And by God's grace, I lost my life in order that I might find true life in Christ.' That life, and the joy of it, spilled over into the founding of Prison Fellowship, which works with prisoners and their families in over a hundred countries around the world.

LOVE OBEYS. The Lord is no tyrant arbitrarily demanding submission to his every whim. Far from it. We cannot enjoy a game if we do not accept its laws, or music if we do not follow its rules. It is a paradox; the more we submit, the more we are free! There is no greater motive for our obedience than his love, and the more we grasp that Christ died for us the more we will love him and want to live for him. The Bible sums it up with, 'This is love for God: to obey his commands.'[6]

'Jesus is Lord' may mean one thing to someone just beginning to follow Christ and something different to another who has been longer on the road. It may be both easier and harder. Harder because there are unforeseen challenges and tougher temptations; easier because experience deepens and relationship grows.

LOVE GROWS. No loving human relationship can thrive without closeness, and as many find, closeness is maintained as much by duty as by longing. At times our spirit may cry out 'My soul thirsts for God …',[7] and at times only a sense of duty brings us to prayer. Faith grows and love deepens when we keep close to God. The output of life needs an input without which the soul dries out, and that input is both personal and communal.

MEMO

The output … needs an input …

PERSONAL

o **Time.** How we manage our time determines our maturity as Christians. Three hours' television a day and a couple of minutes' prayer is no recipe for growth. Time needs to be carved out daily and kept carefully. Gordon MacDonald in *A Resilient Life* writes of himself, 'It is not that every morning is a rapturous experience, but the collective of the mornings, day after day, builds the spirit and makes it a dwelling place for the Lord.' Prayer and the Bible are central as we cultivate closeness.

○ **Bible.** We read with the 'double vision' of understanding and applying. We ask, as many do, if there are 'commands to obey, examples to follow, sins to avoid, promises to claim'. When we read the Word of God, we 'listen' for the Spirit of God to direct us. Sometimes we will memorise as well as meditate, so we have a store of strength to draw on in times of perplexity or temptation.

There is, of course, a wealth of other books to learn from, and many find that their spiritual appetite grows as they read how God has worked in the lives of others.

○ **Prayer.** 'The very act of kneeling,' said one, 'which is so different from everything else I do in the day, helps me worship.' Another says, 'If I kneel I nod off to sleep!' Some sit quietly, others stand or walk. Hands folded or extended, arms raised, eyes closed or open. Some pray lying down looking up, others prostrate themselves before God.

There is worship that may be wordless or clothed in the words of a psalm or in hymns sung silently in the heart. There will be asking for ourselves and for others; for strength in temptation, help in making right choices, courage to be different, new ways in which to serve God, forgiveness for what was done or left undone. And always, always, there will be thanking.

COMMUNAL

It has often been said that if we ever find a perfect church we should not join it, because as soon as *we* join, it will cease to be perfect! Imperfect though we are we need each other, and more than fifty times in the New Testament the words 'one another' and 'each other' appear. The Bible knows nothing of solitary

Christianity and says, 'Let's see how inventive we can be in encouraging love and helping out, not avoiding worshiping together as some do but spurring each other on …'[8] In the church we find –

- **Strength.** Bombarded by the latest products that promise happiness, and sexual images which offer bliss, it is good to be reminded regularly of the call of God upon our lives, to remember that values matter more than things and to recall where true joy is found.

- **Depth.** Knowledge itself does not bring maturity, but maturity never comes through ignorance. We need to learn, and we do that *from* others who have been there before us, and *with* others with whom we share a common bond in Christ.

- **Warmth**. Confronted by apathy to the gospel or experiencing loneliness in a crowd, we find support in the fellowship of our sisters and brothers. One person put it, 'As I warm my hands at a fire so I warm my heart on their faith and love.'

John Newton, once a slave trader, later a minister of the gospel and author of 'Amazing Grace', was a passionate lover of Christ. Towards the end of his life he said, 'I am not what I ought to be; I am not what I wish to be; I am not what I hope to be; but I can truly say, I am not what I once was.' He was a man with an undivided heart.

Called to serve

Those whom Jesus invites to 'come' in faith he also commissions to 'go' in service. It is not enough to stay snugly in the safe immunity of home or church; there is work to be done in the world and a witness to be borne. The words of Jesus, 'let your light shine before men'[9] give an awesome responsibility, which we fulfil by –

o **What we say.** The most natural thing is to share good news. In the Bible we read that Andrew spoke to his brother Simon and 'brought him to Jesus'.[10] Philip told Nathaniel about him and said, 'Come and see'.[11] It was invitation without compulsion. There needs to be an openness about the gospel that respects people's feelings, but not a sensitivity so great that we are silent. Jesus taught in the Sermon on the Mount that 'God is not a secret to be kept. We're going public with this, as public as a city on a hill. If I make you light-bearers, you don't think I'm going to hide you under a bucket, do you?' [12]

A Christian student, who shared accommodation with a friend, told how when the day of graduation came his colleague asked, 'Why is it that during all our time together you never spoke to me about Christ?' He answered, 'Because I thought you didn't care.' 'Didn't care?' said his friend. 'There has never been a day I did not want you to speak, never a night I did not hope you would speak.' It was a turning point in the life of that student who learned to combine courage and courtesy and brought many to Christ.

o **What we are.** Nothing deters people from following Christ more than inconsistency and nothing is more compelling that the attraction of a changed life. One man declared roundly, 'I know that Christ is alive because I see him living in my friends.' Another said of his parents, 'From whose lips I first heard of Jesus, and in whose lives I first saw him.'

o **What we do.** Service may be as visible as one who leads in church or as unnoticed as one who keeps the building clean. For one person service might be overseas, for another it could be going down the road to help the disabled or housebound. There may be a task to be done which is inconvenient or distasteful, so that the natural reaction is 'Why me?' – a question to which one woman responded firmly with, '*Somebody* has to do it; why *not* me?'

Not only are there tasks to be done, there are gifts to be used. How do we identify our gifts? We do so through the counsel of experienced and wise people, but also by experimenting. A young man felt God was calling him to preach, and so prepared four talks against the eventuality that he might be asked to speak. He said later that when that did happen he was so nervous that he used up all four talks in eight minutes. But the gift was there, and in time the world knew that Billy Graham had the gift of the evangelist.

o **What we give.** A man who gave away billions admitted, 'My gift is nothing.' Why? Because he could live on less than one per cent of his wealth. We need to ask ourselves what gap there is between what we give and what we *could* give. Giving can be to the needy, to the church, to the spread of the gospel around the world, and it is not limited to money. It can be in time and skills (see 'Gifts that change lives', page 115). But whatever the nature of our giving we remember that Jesus said, 'You are far happier giving than getting.' [13]

John Wesley summed up our service with, 'Do all the good you can, by all the means you can, in all the ways you can, in all the places you can, at all the times you can, to all the people you can, as long as ever you can.' And John Stott reminds us, 'When we forget ourselves in the self-giving service of love, then joy and peace come flooding into our lives as incidental, unlooked-for blessings', and to the faithful servant is the eventual welcome, 'Come and share your master's happiness!' [14]

Under attack

Even when faith, love and service for Christ are central to us, it does not mean we are immune from attack. But we can –

o **Be encouraged.** We are not alone, for even Jesus was 'tempted in every way, just as we are'.[15] We can overcome, for '... God will never let you down; he'll never let you be pushed past your limit; he'll always be there to help you come through it'.[16] Every temptation to do wrong is also an opportunity to do right, so a temptation overcome can be a step towards growth.

o **Avoid the situation.** 'Avoid the situation as much as the sin itself' are amongst the wisest words ever written. In Proverbs we see a man 'going down the street ... in the direction of her house'.[17] He fell into the sin because he put himself into the situation. Jesus said, 'Stay alert; be in prayer so you don't wander into temptation without even knowing you're in danger'.[18]

> ## 'Avoid the situation as much as the sin itself'
>
> **MEMO**

Pornography is a plague. Because it is so easily accessible on the internet, many put a filter on their computer, for they find it easier to *stay out* of temptation than *get out* of it.

o **Watch for the HALT signs.** It is well said that when we are Hungry, Angry, Lonely or Tired we are more vulnerable to temptation. Let's watch for the HALT signs.

o **Provide for the soul.** An undernourished person will easily fall, and many have found that 'seven prayerless days make one weak'! Let prayer and the Bible be part of our day – every day. That's where strength lies. The psalmist said, 'I have hidden your word in my heart that I might not sin against you.'[19] A man whose difficult job meant many temptations explained, 'I would never have survived but for the complete habit of the quiet time.'

o **Consider the consequences.** The wisdom of Stanley Jones, missionary to India, reminds us that, 'You can make your own choices; you cannot control the consequences of those choices'. The very sin that grieves the Lord, may also impact our life in ways we had not guessed, and have a fall-out over which we have no control.

MEMO

The secret is not in fighting the thought but changing the channel

o **Switch the focus.** Many have proved the truth of 'the expulsive power of a new affection'. The more in love with Christ we are, the less attractive sin becomes. A resounding 'Yes!' to him makes 'No!' to temptation much easier. It is a matter of both commitment and focus. The more we say, 'I mustn't think of pink elephants', the more we will think of them, for what gets our attention gets us. The secret is not in fighting the thought but changing the channel.

MEMO

In openness there is strength and in secrecy weakness

o **Be accountable.** Accountability may not always be necessary or even possible but at times it can be helpful. One evening a man faced with a powerful temptation phoned a friend, told him the situation and added, 'When we talk in the morning please ask me what happened this evening.' He knew that in openness there is strength and in secrecy weakness. Being accountable made him strong.

NOTES

1. Mark 8:36–37
2. Luke 15:24
3. Matthew 28:20
4. Mark 12:30
5. Matthew 5:11–12
6. 1 John 5:3
7. Psalm 42:2
8. Hebrews 10:24–25, *The Message*
9. Matthew 5:16
10. John 1:42
11. John 1:46
12. Matthew 5:14–15, *The Message*
13. Acts 20:35, *The Message*
14. Matthew 25:21
15. Hebrews 4:15
16. 1 Corinthians 10:13, *The Message*
17. Proverbs 7:8
18. Matthew 26:41, *The Message.*
19. Psalm 119:11

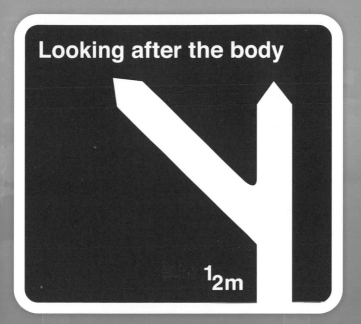

Looking after the body

¹2m

eat with purpose; mind over muscle; when rest is best; dealing with drugs

Looking after the body

Some lavish care on their bodies as if they believed that a perfect body is *the* recipe for happiness. Others are careless to a degree that amounts to abuse. But there is a happy medium. The way we look after our bodies affects our quality of life, and years can be added to (or subtracted from) our lives. The same Bible which stresses the importance of the spiritual, reminds us of the physical, and that 'your body is a sacred place'.[1]

'Listen to your body', we're advised. Well, that depends. If it says, 'Slow down a bit; you're doing too much', that may be good advice. But if we hear it say, 'I want a hamburger, chips and coke five days a week', then we had better not listen. How do we look after our body?

Eat with purpose

Eating is one of the great pleasures of life but it can harm health as well as help it.

ALL ABOUT BALANCE. Forget crash diets. They seldom work, never last and we can end up having more weight and less shape than when we started. Here are some steps to healthy eating.

o **Go for variety.** It's OK to have favourite foods but it's good to try new foods and new ways of preparing them. There is good nutritional evidence behind the rule of thumb, 'The more colour on the plate the better for the body.'

- **Check our intake.** When we eat more than our body needs for energy, the surplus is converted to fat and leads to weight gain. If we have a sedentary lifestyle we should eat less, and as we grow older we need less. We *don't* have to clear our plate. If we weigh ourselves regularly, then weight, with all its health risks, doesn't creep up on us while we are not looking.

- **Eat fruit and vegetables.** 'The healthy way of five a day' is well established. The beauty of fresh fruit and vegetables is they make us feel full but add comparatively few calories, and being high in fibre and rich in antioxidants they are about as healthy as we can get. We don't have to stop at five; the more the healthier.

- **Focus on fibre.** That's fruit and vegetables again and wholegrain products, beans, nuts and seeds – low in calories and rich in vitamins and minerals.

- **Don't be too refined!** Refined carbohydrates like white flour, white bread, polished rice and 'added sugar' products should be avoided. Non-diet soft drinks have loads of calories and no nutrition. Sugar in tea or coffee? 'All my life,' said one, 'I had sugar in coffee and when I stopped it took me ten months to change my taste. But I did it. If someone put sugar in my coffee now I couldn't drink it.'

- **Don't get saturated!** We cut down on saturated fats by choosing low-fat dairy products and lean meat. In cooking we can use vegetable oils and try grilling rather than frying. Fats have double the calories of carbohydrates or proteins. A man with a cake and chocolate weakness, warned off them for health reasons, and no longer keeping them in the house, says, 'I don't honestly miss them and have proved to myself that attitude affects appetite.'

o **Think about drink.** Alcohol is packed with calories so we need to think about drink. Many people find that the more alcohol goes in, the more pounds and inches go on!

MEMO

'Attitude affects appetite'

WHAT GOOD FOOD DOES. Motorists have bought fuel for their car because it was convenient and cheap, not knowing that substances had been added illegally. The price looked good for the pocket but the fuel turned out to be bad for the engine. It didn't run well and finally gave up. It is like that with our body. 'Fast foods' are fat foods. They may be convenient, but if they are bad for the body they are not cheap.

o **Food affects mood.** The food we eat affects the brain. *Alertness* seems boosted by foods with a significant amount of protein, including fish, poultry, meat, eggs, legumes, cheese and milk. *A sense of calm* is linked with eating carbohydrates like wholegrain breads, wholegrain pasta, cereal, rice and fruit. Tests have shown that children of equal ability *perform better* at school and are *happier* when they eat healthy food.

MEMO

Food affects mood

o **Food provides energy.** Athletes and people involved in sport have learned that eating carbohydrates is good preparation for their event or game because they are easy to digest and good for endurance.

○ **Food protects against disease.** There is ample evidence that nuts and berries, dark green vegetables like spinach and broccoli, tomato products, fish, soya and garlic, all help to combat cancer and heart disease. And who would have guessed that good old tea (especially green tea) is a healthy drink rich in antioxidants.

HAZARDS TO HEALTH. If we are significantly overweight, especially over a substantial period of time, we are increasingly vulnerable to a wide variety of medical disorders. Obese people are more likely to develop varicose veins and back pain, and to have skin problems particularly where folds of skin rub together, to develop osteoarthritis and to have high blood pressure and cholesterol. The risk of dying from coronary heart disease and getting type 2 diabetes leaps upwards. The incidence of strokes is doubled and gallstones are more common. There is less energy, more sexual problems and a heavy person falling is more likely to be injured.

Mind over muscle

BENEFITS OF EXERCISE. Fitness starts in the mind. We may not feel like exercise, but if we go for it, gradually the *will to do it* becomes a *want to do it*. Why? Because apart from the enjoyment, the benefits far outweigh the effort, and regular exercise helps us –

The *will to do it* becomes a *want to do it*

MEMO

○ **Feel good.** The feel-good factor is not imagination, for exercise increases the flow of blood and oxygen around the body, and the endorphins released help block pain, reduce stress and enhance self-esteem.

People say over and over, 'I felt so tired I nearly didn't go. But after the exercise I felt great, and far less tired than when I went out.'

o **Control weight.** Exercise burns calories and the more calories we burn the more we control both weight and figure. That boosts confidence and prevents the embarrassment and danger of obesity.

o **Improve posture.** Stronger spinal and abdominal muscles improve flexibility and posture. That helps us stand and walk better, which in turn makes back pain less likely.

o **Sleep better.** Many say, 'When I exercise regularly I go to sleep more quickly, sleep more deeply and wake up fresher.'

o **Strengthen bones.** Exercise increases the mineral content of bones and so reduces the risk of osteoporosis developing, with the greater likelihood of fractures later in life.

o **Combat disease.** When people take regular exercise the risk of diabetes, heart disease, strokes and some cancers is significantly reduced.

o **Live longer.** No one can predict how long they will live, but statistics show that fit people outlive the unfit by a number of years, and those years are more likely to be healthy, productive and enjoyable.

PLAN OF ATTACK. If we are involved in sport on a regular basis then we will probably already be in a healthy routine of practice and training. But if not, then we need a plan of attack.

o **Getting started.** If we haven't been active for some time, or are pregnant, elderly or have health problems, it is wise to check first with a doctor. It makes sense to start slowly, and gradually increase how hard and long we exercise. It's normal to be a little breathless or tired (if we are putting effort into it we ought to be) but we should not be exhausted or gasping for air. At this stage we are not going for gold, we are just getting going. The marathon can wait!

o **What to aim at.** Aerobic exercise is usually defined as any physical activity which can be performed continuously for at least twelve minutes. It's best to choose something we enjoy, or feel we might enjoy, so we regard it as pleasure not punishment. A good aim is to have thirty-minute periods of exercise three times a week. Some may want to do more but any exercise is better than none. The secret of success is regularity.

o **Getting advice.** If we are not sure how to go about exercising we might join a gym where there will be someone to guide us. Some hire a personal trainer. Books and DVDs will not do the walking, running, swimming or dancing for us, but will show us exercises for flexibility and strength. Or we can turn to friends and ask, 'What works for you?'

o **Monitoring progress.** If we write down what we are doing – date, time, distance, lengths, whatever – it becomes as much a celebration of what we have achieved as a reminder of what we are aiming at. A man said, 'For me the habit of recording helps the habit of exercising more than anything else.' For basic fitness there is no need to push the body too far. Exercise is not meant to be painful, so it's all right to stop if it hurts. As we build endurance it doesn't matter if there are times when we have to ease off a little. Later we can pick up our programme again until our fitness improves.

o **Sticking with it.** Many find it more fun exercising with others, and joining a club may lead to friendship as well as 'stickability'. By varying our routine or engaging in other activities we reduce the risk of boredom or injury. A man in his fifties said, 'I found if you want to be fit don't listen to feelings! Just get out and do it.' By gradually building up the distance he walked, he amazed himself by eventually walking fifty miles in one day.

When rest is best

The story of the donkey and peasant has a modern ring. The donkey with a huge stack of firewood strapped to its back, is being driven uphill by the peasant beating the animal unmercifully. It staggers under the load and the beating, and finally sinks to the ground exhausted. As it lies there, the peasant beats it again and again. He beat it *until* it collapsed and then beat it *for* collapsing.

o **Beating ourselves.** That can be the story of our lives. Embarrassed that people might think we are not busy, or inwardly ashamed that we are not, we drive ourselves until we collapse physically, emotionally or spiritually. Then we beat ourselves for collapsing. Things that would normally have been a pleasure become a burden, and life a duty without joy. The Bible says that God 'rested'.[2] Did he need to? No, but he chose to. We need to, and often choose not to. But the rhythm of work and rest is fundamental to a healthy life. Even the heart rests between beats, and time away from work is not wasted.

MEMO

We drive ourselves until we collapse ... Then we beat ourselves for collapsing

○ **What's rest?** Rest is not necessarily inactivity but a change in activity. It depends on lifestyle. There is a rule about rest – if mind tires, use muscles; if muscles tire, use mind. So for a person in a sedentary occupation, being physically active can be part of resting, while a person working manually may find mental stimulation restful.

> **If mind tires, use muscles; if muscles tire, use mind**
>
> MEMO

○ **Getting the balance.** Rest is about balance. Not only does work need rest, rest needs work. It is possible to wake up in the morning feeling weary because there is no meaningful work to look forward to. For the most part rest is a healthy choice, but it can become an unhealthy demand when a lazy person does so little that mind and muscle atrophy. They are alive but not living.

IMPORTANCE OF SLEEP

Food, air and sleep are the three absolute essentials for life. A very few people get by with four hours' sleep a night, and some need ten, but most average seven or eight. As road accidents show, skimping on sleep can be dangerous, with sleep loss having effects similar to drinking excessive amounts of alcohol. Sleep is important but focusing too much on it is counter-productive. Worrying about it can keep us awake.

○ **Sheep and sleep.** There are ways to get good sleep without visiting doctor or chemist. Sleeping pills can cause dependence, and when a person takes them for some time they may experience withdrawal symptoms when stopping. As for counting sheep, a would-be sleeper put it, 'I never was good at arithmetic and the concentration needed for counting keeps me awake. For me sheep and sleep don't mix.'

o **Night follows day.** How we sleep is influenced by how we live; by our lifestyle as well as by what happens during the day. Stress is one of the main inhibitors of sleep, but fortunately there are ways of dealing with it (see 'Stress and de-stress', page 30). Exercise and a healthy diet, cutting out smoking and cutting down caffeine and alcohol, all contribute to a good night's sleep. The fitter we are the better we sleep.

o **Power naps.** Some find it helps to have a post-lunch nap. Concentration, productivity and relating can all be improved by it. That's fine so long as it is short enough not to affect our sleep at night.

o **Slow down for sleep.** We prepare ourselves best for sleep by doing whatever we find relaxing. Routines help body and brain get ready for sleep and they respond better to a regular rhythm, including going to bed at much the same time each night.

o **Going to sleep.** A firm mattress is better than a soft one, and we fall asleep faster if our hands and feet are warm. If sleep doesn't come easily then rather than tossing and turning, many people use one or more of the three 'r's (reading, radio and relaxing – even if it means getting out of bed for a 'cupper'). And a pad beside the bed for the 'mustn't forget that' thought which would keep us awake.

Dealing with drugs

ILLEGAL DRUGS. It's only a small pill or capsule, a bit of powder, what looks like a piece of paper with a picture on it. It's not a needle; there's nothing to worry about. Or is there? The road into drugs is easy, the road out hard, and some never make it.

What are the facts and consequences?

- **Facts.** Uppers (stimulants) raise levels of activity in the body and make a person feel more alert and energetic (cocaine, crack, ecstasy, amphetamines such as speed).

  Downers (depressants) slow bodily processes and make a person less aware (cannabis and opiates such as heroin).

  Psychedelics (hallucinogens) distort the senses and perceptions (LSD, magic mushrooms). Cannabis can have hallucinogenic as well as depressant effects.

- **Consequences.** Supply or even possession can attract fines or imprisonment, and the penalties for driving under the influence of drugs are the same as driving under the influence of alcohol. Negative effects include impaired judgment, loss of memory and co-ordination, breathing problems, blurred vision, seizures and death. Long-term effects include cancers, heart problems and kidney failure. The sharing of needles and syringes risk HIV/AIDS and Hepatitis B and C. Addiction, the almost inevitable outcome of drug use, needs money to feed the habit, money often obtained through theft, fraud, violence and prostitution.

TOBACCO. Of all the millions in the world who have smoked for years, most wish they had never started.

- **Addiction.** Nicotine is a highly addictive drug and few people are occasional smokers. Surveys show that over eighty per cent of teenagers who smoke become addicted. 'Smoking kills' printed on cigarette packets is not just scare mongering, for between a third and a half of people who smoke for a lifetime will die a smoking-related death.

- **Diseases.** Smokers are more likely to get pneumonia, emphysema and chronic bronchitis, strokes, heart attacks, coronary heart disease and many cancers. Lung cancer is about nine times more common in smokers than non-smokers. Premature wrinkling of the skin is more likely with smokers, who also have a higher risk of blindness, infertility in women and impotence in men. When a mother continues to smoke during the first year of her baby's life, the child is more likely to get croup, pneumonia, bronchitis and meningitis.

- **Costs.** Two twenty-a-day smokers will in their lifetime smoke approximately the value of an average-priced home in the United Kingdom.

ALCOHOL. It is an addictive drug. Tolerance increases with use, dependence can creep up and vulnerability varies from person to person. Not everyone drinks alcohol, but for those who do the Department of Health advises that men should not have more than three to four units in a day, and women no more than two to three units in a day (one pint of ordinary strength beer or glass of wine = two units; one pub measure of spirits = one unit). But it is also recommended that there should be a day or days in the week when no alcohol at all is used. There is, of course, *no* 'safe level' of alcohol, for a single glass can begin a habit which may spiral out of control.

- **Health.** Long-term effects of alcohol abuse include heart disease, strokes, many cancers, cirrhosis of the liver, alcoholic poisoning and mental health problems.

- **Violence.** Alcohol contributes to forty per cent of violent crime and eighty per cent of criminal damage. It is a factor in a third of domestic violence incidents, and its misuse identified in fifty per cent of child protection cases.

- **Sex.** Young people are many times less likely to use condoms regularly where there is a pattern of alcohol and sex, thus greatly increasing unwanted pregnancies and sexual infections.

- **Accidents.** Alcohol is a major contributor to deaths on the road for drivers, passengers and other road users. A third of admissions to hospital A&E departments are alcohol related.

Let's not minimise the effect that our body has on the rest of our life, and let us treat it with respect and discipline. The apostle Paul, writing of both body and spirit, said, 'No sloppy living for me! I'm staying alert and in top condition'.[3] A life motto doesn't come better than this.

NOTES

1. 1 Corinthians 6:19, *The Message*
2. Exodus 20:11
3. 1 Corinthians 9:27, *The Message*

Relating to others

12m

respecting each other; friendship;
family matters; gifts that change
lives; en*courage*ment

Relating to others

Mind, feelings and character; spirit and body; the parts make the whole. But we exist in a world, not a vacuum. How do we relate to others in our world? The words of Jesus often known as the Golden Rule, '… do to others what you would have them do to you …',[1] define behaviour as nothing else does.

Respecting each other

o **Self-respect.** Self-esteem is not to be confused with selfishness, but is the way in which we see ourselves. We fail, but refuse the label of failure; we succeed, but do not boast. A healthy self-esteem acknowledges that we matter, but not more or less than others. Being at ease with ourselves is self-respect, and those who respect themselves are more likely to show respect to others – and be easier to live and work with.

RESPECTING OTHERS. Their feelings are just as important to them as ours are to us, and we need to be sensitive as to how they think and feel. We should –

NEVER
o *Ridicule* or deliberately embarrass anyone. Names, sarcasm or jokes carelessly made, leave scars that last a lifetime.
o *Bully.* Even a one-off incident hurts, but continued bullying is devastating. A woman who suffered constant harassment in her office had a serious breakdown. A boy said, 'I would rather die than go back to school.'
o *Use violence,* though there are times when it may

be necessary to use force defending ourselves
or others. The consequences of violence are
unpredictable and, apart from injury, may bring about
the loss of friends, family, liberty and even life.

o *Make offensive remarks* about race, religion, sex,
age or colour, or about people who are handicapped
in any way.

ALWAYS

o *Listen with care.* We should try to understand what is
said to us. Asking questions shows we are listening.
o *Be tolerant* of minor faults or flaws in other people.
We have a few of our own!
o *Be courteous.* The words 'please' and 'thank you'
make our part of the world a warmer place to live in.
o *Be considerate.* Picture in our mind how what we do
(or don't do) might affect others.
o *Apologise* when we believe we have caused hurt.

RESPECT DIFFERENCES IN GENDER

There are differences which are characteristic of men
and of women, but none is absolute. In general a man
needs to feel significant and that he is adequate and
respected, whereas a woman needs to feel secure, that
she is loved, understood and cared for.

For many women (not all) talking is part of the
thinking process. Their words express possibilities
rather than conclusions. They sort as they talk. But for
many men self-talk in the head leads to conclusions
before they speak. It might even be said that women
think aloud and men talk silently!

RESPECT DIFFERENCES IN PERSONALITY

Just as each person has two hands but prefers to use
one more than the other, so everyone is objective and
subjective but tends to be more of one – maybe ninety
per cent more.

Here are a few characteristics. What matters is not the differences but our acceptance of them.

> **MEMO**
>
> ## What matters is not the differences but our acceptance of them

- One likes order and structure, another goes with the flow
- One decides with the head, another with the heart
- One goes step by step, another jumps in anywhere
- One is at ease with the measurable, another with possibilities
- One acts on facts, another on hunches
- One is passionate about principles, another about relationships
- One is sociable, another reserved

RESPECT PERSONAL DIFFERENCES

A husband and wife laugh at their 'irreconcilable differences'. In the evening when it begins to get dark and the light in the sitting room is switched on, he wants to close the curtains. He explains, 'I don't want people looking in and seeing me.' His wife is the opposite. She says, 'The day is short enough and I like to see the street lights and passing cars.' What do they do? In his words, 'We pull the curtains part of the way. I can hide behind them and she can sit where she can see!' Compromise (in the best sense) is interwoven with respect.

The Bible shows the importance of our attitude and treatment of others in the words, 'Show proper respect to everyone …'[2]

Friendship

Friendship is a major factor in happiness as loneliness is in unhappiness. Human beings are made for relationship, but there is not time in one life to be a friend to everyone. But where we can't be a friend, we can still be friendly, with a ready smile, a direct look, an attentive ear and a word of thanks. From friendliness, friendship may spring.

MAKING FRIENDS. Friendships start by –

- **Common interests.** Children are thrown together by school or by their parent's friends, but gradually they are drawn together by things they have in common; interests, tastes and values. It is the same in the adult world, thrown together by work, involvements or neighbourhood, drawn together by choice.

- **Doing something.** The doggerel has it, 'Don't sit on your bum and expect them to come.' We need to go places, do things, get involved and, even if it doesn't come naturally at first, make up our minds to meet and talk with people. We might not click immediately with this one or that one, but we keep ourselves open to making friends. We may (with care) get in touch with people on the internet.

- **Being a friend.** The best way to find friends is to be one. There are people out there coming apart at the seams and crying out for friendship. *We* may meet their need as well as our own. A woman admitted, 'I never saw myself as a friendly kind of person, but when I made the running, people came running.'

BEING FRIENDS. What makes for good friendship?

- **Time.** We can work with people for years and never become friends. It's easy to have time without friendship, but hard to have friendship without time. If our friends are at a distance, we keep in contact by letter, text, phone or computer. If they are close at hand we do the same, but we also spend time *with* them. It may be a meal, a coffee, shopping or a game, in church or community, a walk and talk, but in a word it's – time. The amount of time evolves so that meeting with them is a pleasure for both and a pressure for neither.

o **Openness.** Friendship is two-way; it gives and receives.

Sharing. We feel safe in sharing things about ourselves which we would never normally disclose. We can talk about hopes and failures, dreams and disappointments, and feel 'lighter' because we feel understood. Our openness makes it easier for our friend to be open too, for in a deep sense freedom begets freedom, and we experience what psychiatrist John White says: 'Pain shared is pain divided, pleasure shared is pleasure multiplied.'

MEMO 'Pain shared is pain divided, pleasure shared is pleasure multiplied'

Confidentiality. Trust leads to openness and openness to trust, and that is an important part of happiness, for trusting and being trusted adds strength to life. But the trusted must be trustworthy. Nothing destroys a friendship more than a 'leaking bucket' through which private things seep out.

Frankness. Openness can lead to frankness. A woman confessed, 'I hoped you wouldn't say that, but I'm glad you did! Thank you for being straight with me. I needed to hear that.' Frankness with sensitivity is a gift of close friendship.

- **Caring.** It has been said that some people 'bring joy wherever they go; others bring joy *when* they go'. Some are invigorating, others exhausting. What makes the difference? Caring! They listen, talk with us, laugh with us, cry with us. They are fun to be with. They may be busy, but they don't hurry. Their heart has large rooms. 'Carry each other's burdens'[3] is what they do. They are not fair-weather friends, and if one falls the other is there to help him up. Being with them warms the heart; from that warmth love may grow.

- **Acceptance.** Friends don't judge, they listen, and are better at picking up pieces than throwing stones. Acceptance doesn't necessarily mean approval, for it's still true that, 'a friend is one who knows the worst about you and loves you just the same'. The famous psychiatrist, Dr Paul Tournier, said that people were often disappointed when they wanted to study his methods because, and he explained, 'I have no methods. All I do is accept people.'

> **Friends ... are better at picking up pieces than throwing stones**
>
> MEMO

- **Affirmation.** Affirmation not only *confirms* character ('I admire your kindness, your honesty, your consideration') but helps *create* it, for when people feel appreciated and valued, they say in the depths of their being, 'I want to be *more* of what you see me to be.'

FRIENDSHIP ENDING. However meaningful a friendship is, not many last a lifetime. Why?

- **Drifting apart.** Friendships fade as the school gates close for the last time and young people grow up and go in different directions. Further study, job change or new relationships mean there are new interests. Adults themselves move on with commitments of work or family, or because of time and distance one-time friends drift apart.

o **Withdrawing**. Some friendships fade, others are severed by –

Conflict. A word out of place, a misunderstanding, a 'position' that must be defended, and two friends find that 'big walls are made from little bricks'. Once the wall is up it can be hard to take down. If in spite of every effort the relationship cannot be restored, let's choose to hold good memories from the past rather than bad.

Values. A woman felt tremendous pressure to engage in a lifestyle that she felt was wrong. She said, 'I felt myself drowning in values I did not own,' and added, 'It was either their way or what I believed was right. The choice was difficult, but easy.'

FRIENDSHIP IN A NUTSHELL. Friendship blunts our pain and boosts our happiness. Francis Bacon knew all about it four hundred years ago when he summed up friendship with, 'It redoubleth joys; and cutteth griefs in halves.'

Family matters

MARRIAGE

The recipe for a happy marriage is found in the acronym CAREFUL (see outline on the next page), which the authors have used in their book *The Highway Code for Marriage* (CWR, 2005). Without care the house becomes a ruin, the garden a wilderness, the farm unproductive, the business a failure. For a marriage to thrive it needs ongoing care.

Communication. The happily married make time to talk, take care to listen and find it is possible to disagree without being disagreeable.

Affection. Some find it difficult to show affection, but it is a learned art. The verbal, physical and sexual combine to warm and enrich their marriage.

Respect. Respect begins with self-respect and says, 'What's important to him (or her) is important whether I understand it or not.' It brings dignity to marriage.

Encouragement. Good partners scrap the failure list and are generous with praise. They create an atmosphere of affirmation and an attitude of gratitude.

Forgiveness. Forgiveness takes strength, is more choice than feeling, and sets a couple free to build or rebuild their relationship.

Unselfishness. Happiness lies with two people who have the one purpose of pleasing each other. Time, money and responsibilities are shared.

Loyalty. The unswerving commitment of wife and husband means that they will avoid situations or friendships which might endanger their marriage.

In a good marriage husband and wife see themselves as a team and put the good of the team first. He makes her problems his. She is glad when he does well. They put 'we' before 'me', and what is good for the team is good for both members of it. Good marriages don't just happen – they are made.

Good marriages don't just happen – they are made

MEMO

PARENTING

To *become* a parent we need no licence, take no exam, pass no test. But *being* a parent is the most challenging and rewarding job in the world. The *person* we are influences more than anything else the *parent* we become. The ABC below is a summary of the authors' book *The Highway Code for Parenting* (CWR, 2007).

Absorbing love. Children are sponges absorbing parental love. That love is safe, thoughtful, honest and giving. It sets limits and it protects. Above all love is spelt TIME.

Building their self-esteem. When children feel loved, accepted and adequate, they grow a healthy self-esteem. The words 'I'm proud of you' work wonders.

Choosing to discipline. Love is not the opposite of discipline but the chief reason for it. Love must often say, 'No. I care about the way you grow up.'

Developing character. When parents teach faith, integrity and sexual standards, they must remember that children identify as much (or more) with their parents' behaviour as with their words.

Equipping for life. It's a tough world out there and children need to learn not only about manners and money, but also how to stay safe from dangerous things and people.

Facing big issues. Pressured to do drugs a teenager replied, 'Open-minded? That's why I said "No". I want a mind to be open-minded with!'

Gaining maturity. Children need roots and wings, and parents must learn to be available but not exploited, supportive but not intrusive and loving but not demanding.

Being a mother or father is a responsibility like no other, and with each child there is only one chance to get it right. It is literally true that 'the opportunity of a lifetime must be taken within the lifetime of the opportunity'.

Gifts that change lives

Some of the best-known words in the world are '…
Love your neighbour as yourself.'[4] From the parable of
the Good Samaritan[5] it is clear that 'love' doesn't mean
affection (the man in the story was a stranger) but a
duty of care, and 'neighbour' (for the same reason) is
not just the person next door but fellow human beings.
Everyone has responsibilities that include –

> … 'the opportunity of a lifetime must be taken within the lifetime of the opportunity'
>
> MEMO

MONEY. A man said, 'I love money', and he went on to
explain, 'It can go to parts of the world I will never be
able to go to. It doesn't have to spend years learning
a language or adjusting to climate or culture. It never
tires, never gets ill and cannot die. It brings clean water
to the thirsty, health to the sick and knowledge to those
who have never been to school. Above all it can bring
faith, hope and love. Yes, I love money – for what it can
do.' Our money cannot buy happiness for us, but it can
give happiness to others.

'Make poverty history' has inspired many 'haves'
to help the 'have nots'. But there is much more to do.
The need is not only for basics like food, clothing,
shelter and safe drinking water, but also for education
and affordable health care. Millions are trapped in
a downward spiral by lack of money … lack of food
… lack of health … lack of work … lack of money …
then all over again … lack of food … lack of … so 800
million go to bed hungry and at least 25,000 die daily
from poverty-related causes. It is rightly said that 'If we
lived more simply, others might simply live'.

TIME. There are some who can't give money but few who can't give time. Time to comfort, to care for, to support, to help out, to encourage in a hundred different ways.

An older man gave time mentoring a seemingly hopeless young drug addict who had been in and out of prison. It was hard work. Was the time wasted? No! The old man is gone now but the young man, with life transformed, lives on, helping the hopeless himself. When we give time we give a part of ourselves that we never get back.

SKILLS. A skill acquired by time and training can be an asset which helps a church, lifts a community or transforms the life of an individual. The giving of a skill often saves money and is worth far more than money. People in a village in a developing country walked six hours a day to collect a bucket of water, until an engineer used his skill so the villagers now get their water with the turn of a tap. When he retired, an experienced surgeon gave three months overseas so that a hospital could continue to function while a missionary doctor came home for a much needed break.

To give a skill is one thing, to teach it is another. As the saying goes, 'Give a man a fish and you feed him for a day; teach a man to fish and you feed him for life.'

THINGS. The gift of a bicycle enables a midwife in a developing country to double her home visits in a day. A sewing-machine gives a trade and an income to help a mother feed her family. Books that might be thrown away in the West can open the door to learning in other parts of the world.

ORGAN, TISSUE AND BLOOD DONATION.
Many give their blood, which is used by hospitals in emergencies and operations. Organ donors who look beyond their death or families beyond their grief, save or transform the lives of people they have never known. A father and mother said, 'Nothing and no one can replace our child, but we are glad that one small boy will grow to manhood because he has our son's heart.' Thousands of lives are helped every year by organ and tissue donation, and in some cases several people can benefit from the one donor. In death there can be the gift of life.

In death there can be the gift of life

MEMO

Encouragement

Encouragement warms the heart, lifts the spirit and gives the courage to go on in spite of difficulty. We can't buy it; we can only give it – to the same person over and over again, or to someone we have never met before and may never meet again. When we encourage we get as we give, for we are made kinder by being kind, made stronger by giving strength, and our own heart is warmed as it goes out to another. Scrawled under a railway bridge is the wisdom of a graffiti artist, 'The secret of being happy is doing things for other people.' We encourage and are encouraged by –

o **Smiles.** A woman said, 'I go to that café not just for the coffee but for the smile of the waitress. It warms me all day.' Smiles are better than frowns. They use fewer muscles and as the years go by leave fewer wrinkles!

o **Spoken words.** 'You can do it; I know you can,' were the words one woman said had turned her life around. In a dead end job in a rundown company, poorly housed and 'going nowhere', she was encouraged to retrain herself. Long familiar with rejection and being put down, it was hard to stick at her studies. But she made it in the end and life took on a new dimension. She explained, 'The fact that you believed in me and told me I could do it, changed my life.'

MEMO

'The fact that you believed in me ... changed my life'

- **Written words.** A mature man writing to his parents for their wedding anniversary said, 'Thank you for a lifetime of encouragement, and as life moves on I appreciate all the more the richness of my childhood and the family life we enjoyed together.' That simple sentence became a prized possession. Notes, letters or cards that take minutes to write can be treasured for years.

- **Listening.** Everyone has three ears – a left ear, a right ear and an ear in the middle of the h*ear*t! A person, hurt by harsh words or hard times, draws strength and comfort from us when we listen with all three ears. A man sought out a friend and said afterwards, 'I knew by his eyes he was listening to me, and by the way he listened I knew he cared. It was good to feel understood.'

- **Helping**. An older couple, involved in a road accident, were dependent for months on friends and neighbours to bring them to doctor, hospital and physiotherapist. Their shopping was done for them, food cooked, clothes washed, the grass cut and a wheelchair hired. They were brought to church and even to showrooms as they looked for a car to replace the one that was written off. The couple said, 'You couldn't be down long with friends like that. They were our arms and legs!'

o **Time.** A man writing to his mother on her birthday remembered, 'You were always there … giving us your time', and an anxious student said to her counsellor, 'Thank you for giving me your time.' Time is the most valuable thing we possess and the greatest gift we have. When we give it voluntarily and gladly we are saying in effect, 'You matter.' Let us give it while we have it.

o **Touch.** The wrong kind of touch can be intrusive and abusive, but the absence of wholesome touch can be deeply painful. A woman told how she went to communion in her local church because at the time in the service when it is the custom to greet those nearest with, 'The peace of the Lord be with you', it was always accompanied by a handshake, hug or kiss on the cheek. She explained, 'That is the only time in the week that anyone ever touches me.'

o **Gifts**. There are duty gifts, fun gifts, love gifts and gifts that support a person or advance a cause. Gifts can be received with a groan because they are unnecessary or unwanted, with pleasure because they meet a need, or with joy because the giver is in the gift. A wife, whose husband had been thoughtless, told how she came into the house one day and found a small vase in which there was a solitary dandelion, and a note which humbly asked, 'Will this do for starters?' She was thrilled not by the size of the gift but the warmth of the thought.

o **Kindness.** A man said, 'I ate a bar of chocolate and savoured its rich round taste. I chatted with a lonely man and as I did I saw his eyes lighten and a smile crease his face. When I went to bed, the taste had long since gone, but I could still see the smile. What was the difference? I enjoyed the chocolate but gave joy to the man.' That's it; pleasure is nothing compared with joy, and in kindness there is always joy. Mark Twain said, 'It is the language the deaf can hear and the blind can see.'

o **Friendship.** A person said, 'I am alone and sometimes lonely, but I can lift the phone any day and walk into the warmth of their friendship.' When we give friendship we find that novelist and dramatist James M. Barrie was right when he said, 'Those who bring sunshine into the lives of others, cannot keep it from themselves.' Happiness is found in giving it to others.

MEMO

'Those who bring sunshine into the lives of others, cannot keep it from themselves'

The way we live life and relate to others is summed up best in the words of Jesus:

'Give away your life; you'll find life given back, but not merely given back – given back with bonus and blessing.' [6]

NOTES

1. Matthew 7:12
2. 1 Peter 2:17
3. Galatians 6:2
4. Mark 12:31
5. Luke 10:30–37
6. Luke 6:38, *The Message*

It doesn't just happen

Life is always testing, often difficult, sometimes almost unbearable, but what happens *in us* is more important than what happens *to us*. As we aim to make the best use of our life we find that it is shaped by the attitudes we adopt, the beliefs we hold and the choices we make.

ATTITUDES

Past. Everyone has good and bad memories. The ones we dwell on will determine whether we look back with bitterness or gladness, and will make us either sour or serene. Happy people focus on good events in the past, not the worst.

Present. Everyone has good and bad experiences. We may not be able to control the situations we are in or the actions of others, but we *can* control how we react. Our positive 'happitude' affects how we feel even in the toughest environment.

Future. Everyone has good and bad expectations. Focusing on bad things which *may* happen, makes for worry and weakness; setting our mind on good outcomes makes for hope and happiness.

BELIEFS

Meaning. To 'love the Lord your God with all your heart' and 'your neighbour as yourself', and to live for Christ with an undivided heart, gives meaning to life that nothing else does.

Wholeness. We are meant to be whole; mind and feelings, body and spirit, character and relationships, interacting and influencing each other for good. Life is best when integrated.

Happiness. The longing for happiness is universal but is found, not when it's a goal, but as an outcome of an integrated life and a by-product of unselfishness and service.

Choices

Happiness lies less in demanding rights and more in fulfilling responsibilities; less in self-interest and more in self-control; less in grumbling over difficulties and more in grasping opportunities; less in comfort and more in challenge; less in having and more in sharing; less in getting and more in giving. It is not once-discovered and then 'happily-ever-after'. It requires –

Honesty – that recognises we have strengths, admits we have weaknesses and confesses we need help to turn our lives around.
Courage – for the breaking and making of habits, and the changing of character, lifestyle and relationships.
Perseverance – that guards the gains we make and never gives up.

National Distributors

UK: (and countries not listed below)
CWR, Waverley Abbey House, Waverley Lane, Farnham, Surrey GU9 8EP.
Tel: (01252) 784700 Outside UK (44) 1252 784700

AUSTRALIA: CMC Australasia, PO Box 519, Belmont, Victoria 3216.
Tel: (03) 5241 3288 Fax: (03) 5241 3290

CANADA: David C Cook Distribution Canada, PO Box 98, 55 Woodslee
Avenue, Paris, Ontario N3L 3E5. Tel: 1800 263 2664

GHANA: Challenge Enterprises of Ghana, PO Box 5723, Accra.
Tel: (021) 222437/223249 Fax: (021) 226227

HONG KONG: Cross Communications Ltd, 1/F, 562A Nathan Road, Kowloon.
Tel: 2780 1188 Fax: 2770 6229

INDIA: Crystal Communications, 10-3-18/4/1, East Marredpalli, Secunderabad
– 500026, Andhra Pradesh. Tel/Fax: (040) 27737145

KENYA: Keswick Books and Gifts Ltd, PO Box 10242, Nairobi.
Tel: (02) 331692/226047 Fax: (02) 728557

MALAYSIA: Salvation Book Centre (M) Sdn Bhd, 23 Jalan SS 2/64,
47300 Petaling Jaya, Selangor. Tel: (03) 78766411/78766797 Fax: (03)
78757066/78756360

NEW ZEALAND: CMC Australasia, PO Box 303298, North Harbour,
Auckland 0751. Tel: 0800 449 408 Fax: 0800 449 049

NIGERIA: FBFM, Helen Baugh House, 96 St Finbarr's College Road, Akoka,
Lagos.
Tel: (01) 7747429/4700218/825775/827264

PHILIPPINES: OMF Literature Inc, 776 Boni Avenue, Mandaluyong City.
Tel: (02) 531 2183 Fax: (02) 531 1960

SINGAPORE: Alby Commercial Enterprises Pte Ltd, 95 Kallang Avenue
#04-00, AIS Industrial Building, 339420. Tel: (65) 629 27238 Fax: (65) 629
27235

SOUTH AFRICA: Struik Christian Books, 80 MacKenzie Street, PO Box 1144,
Cape Town 8000. Tel: (021) 462 4360 Fax: (021) 461 3612

SRI LANKA: Christombu Publications (Pvt) Ltd, Bartleet House,
65 Braybrooke Place, Colombo 2. Tel: (9411) 2421073/2447665

TANZANIA: CLC Christian Book Centre, PO Box 1384, Mkwepu Street,
Dar es Salaam. Tel/Fax: (022) 2119439

USA: David C Cook Distribution Canada, PO Box 98, 55 Woodslee Avenue,
Paris, Ontario N3L 3E5, Canada. Tel: 1800 263 2664

ZIMBABWE: Word of Life Books (Pvt) Ltd, Christian Media Centre,
8 Aberdeen Road, Avondale, PO Box A480 Avondale, Harare. Tel: (04) 333355
or 091301188

For email addresses, visit the CWR website: www.cwr.org.uk

CWR is a Registered Charity – Number 294387

**CWR is a Limited Company registered in England – Registration
Number 1990308**

Build - or rebuild - a successful marriage

Discover seven proven secrets to marital joy and fulfilment with this honest and humorous book.

In memorable, bite-sized chunks it will show you how to build a loving, healthy and lasting relationship.

The Highway Code for Marriage
by Michael and Hilary Perrott
128-page paperback, colour throughout
ISBN: 978-1-85345-331-1
Only £6.99

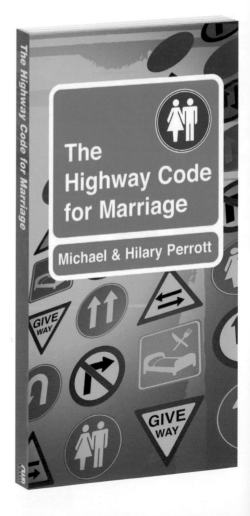

Effective parenting in bite-sized chunks

This humorous guide will help you to:
- Build children's security and self-esteem
- Discipline them lovingly and effectively
- Equip them to deal with bullies, drugs and other issues of life.

Also great for grandparents and carers!

The Highway Code for Parenting
by Michael and Hilary Perrott
112-page paperback, colour throughout
ISBN: 978-1-85345-419-6
Only £6.99

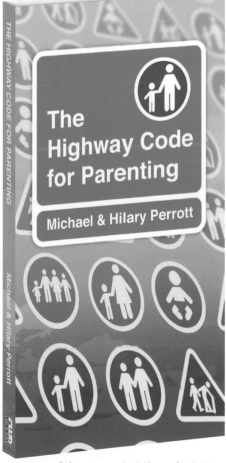

Prices correct at time of printing.

Overcome procrastination

Find out what is behind your tendency to put things off and discover how you *can* change.

- Gain more time, achievement and freedom
- Reduce your frustrations and stress levels
- Increase your efficiency and confidence.

This practical and highly motivating guide will impact on all areas of your life.

Just Do It
by Michael and Hilary Perrott
120-page paperback, colour throughout
ISBN: 978-1-85345-392-2
Only £6.99